W.B. YEATS

His Poetry and Politics

W.B. YEATS

His Poetry and Politics

M.P. Sinha

ATLANTIC
PUBLISHERS & DISTRIBUTORS (P) LTD

Published by

ATLANTIC

PUBLISHERS & DISTRIBUTORS (P) LTD

7/22, Ansari Road, Darya Ganj,
New Delhi-110002
Phones : +91-11-40775252, 23273880, 23275880, 23280451
Fax : +91-11-23285873
Web : www.atlanticbooks.com
E-mail : orders@atlanticbooks.com

Branch Office
5, Nallathambi Street, Wallajah Road,
Chennai-600002
Phones : +91-44-64611085, 32413319
E-mail : chennai@atlanticbooks.com

Printed in India at Glorious Printers, A-13, D.S.I.D.C.,
Jhilmil Industrial Area, Delhi-110095

DEDICATED

In Memory of My Father and Mother
Suresh Prasad Sinha
Chandramukhi Devi
who were
My First Teachers

Preface

Poetry, politics and ideology are closely linked. No poet, no artist can escape the politics of his time. As far as Yeats is concerned, he was actively involved in politics right from the beginning of his poetical career. No doubt, his poetry is marked by esotericism, mysticism and symbolism of a private nature; its substantial part has its roots in politics. For a proper evaluation of his poetry it is pertinent to understand his political ideas and trace the sources of their origin and development.

More significantly, as Karl Marx has theorized, literature is a part of the superstructure of society and is continually determined by man's material activity and mode of production which form the base structure. For a proper study and evaluation of a creative writer we have to define the social structure of the time and analyse the way that exploited class struggles for economic and political freedom.

Ireland, in the nineteenth century, was the exploited class in relation to England. The Irish nationalists struggled for freedom. Yeats, in his early youth, came in contact with the Irish nationalists and, under the influence of John O'Leary, joined the Revolutionary Party—Irish Republican Brotherhood. In the beginning he dreamed of the heroic Ireland of the past but later on grappled with the contemporary reality and wrote a very different kind of poetry, hard and sinewy.

The main objective of poetry is not to give the reader aesthetic pleasure only, but to present reality as it is and enlighten him to solve the problems of life, both material and spiritual. I have analysed Yeats's poetry and politics from this point of view.

All quotations from the primary and secondary sources are from the editions listed in the Selected Bibliography.

I owe my gratitude to Professor Amresh Datta who initiated me to Yeats. I am thankful to Dr. K.R. Gupta, Chairman, Atlantic Publishers and Distributors for printing the book in a short time.

M.P. SINHA

Contents

Introduction

Poetry; politics and ideology (the non-said) are closely linked. Although creative writers have been inspired by political events and have created in their work a world where human misery and suffering can be mitigated, literary critics have either ignored or disparaged this aspect, as if politics and ideology would contaminate poetry. Among the non-Marxist critics, C.M. Bowra is one of the first to deplore this attitude:

> Many people dislike the notion that poetry can have any connection with politics and think that even if we extend politics to cover a whole range of public events, it stands in awkward relation to poetry, that its incursions are usually unsuccessful and often deplorable and that its influence defiles an otherwise pure art.[1]

After analyzing some of the best political poetry of the world (including two poems of Mao-Tse-tung), he arrives at the conclusion:

> Poetry on public events has much right to exist as poetry on the other subject, since it helps us to grasp them without yielding to the numbing influence of lower method of communication.[2]

The difference between my approach and that of Bowra is that whereas Bowra confines himself to poetry written on public events and politicians who have written other kinds of poetry, I am primarily concerned with relationship between poetry, politics and ideology. Again, I differ with the dogmatic Marxist critics who denounce a writer for not following the party line. A great poet is a thinker who goes left to the party line occasionally or when he feels that the party has failed to serve the common people and has become autocratic.

My endeavour in this study is to trace the different influences that shaped Yeats's ideology and explain how his political ideas find expression in his poetry. Most Marxist critics try to seek in a poet's work a scathing criticism of the ruling class and eulogy of the communist rule. It is this kind of prescription by Zhadanov that made Gorky and Mayakovsky frustrated men and Boris Pasternak an exile. The famous Marxist critic Christopher Caudwell oversimplified Karl Marx and denounced Shelley and Byron. Georg Lukacs, perhaps, the greatest critic of his country had to see many ups and downs in his career. The important thing is that a creative writer should be evaluated in the socio-historical context and the critic's task is to discover a poet's position in his class, trace the causes of his suffering and then find out how sincerely he defends the human values in a period of crisis. A great poet, because he rises above his personal and class interests, always considers the world a family and in his work envisions the world of his ideal.

The great majority of critics evade Yeats's politics because they are not clear in their ideology and also because they have not been able to digest his partisan attitude to aristocracy and temporary flirtation with fascism. Yeats should be evaluated not only on the basis of his artistic perfection but also how far his poetry solves man's problems in the universe. A balanced evaluation shall analyse both his positive and negative sides and never ignore his essays, letters, interviews, recollections and autobiography. He was a multi-faceted personality and throughout his life he strove to hammer different elements into a unity. Philosophy, religion, politics and esotericism were all welded into one in his poetry. Although poetry was his main objective but not the ultimate goal; although autonomous, it was a means to achieve Unity of Being and Unity of Culture. He expressed the opinion that a poet must conceive a world of his ideal before writing poetry; otherwise he would confuse his readers:

> In my youth I was accustomed to say that no man should be permitted to open his mouth until he had sung or written his 'Utopia,' for lacking that we could not know where he was taking us, and I still think that artists of all kinds should once again praise or represent great or happy people.[3]

The quoted passage found expression in "Under Ben Bulben," one of his last poems. The idea that a poet should write about the great and happy people is a romantic ideal and takes cue from Shelley's famous sentence that poetry is the expression of the happiest people in the happiest moment. Yeats in his youth wanted to bring Ireland to the level of England and France and this he could do (he wrote on many occasions), by reviving the ancient heroic Ireland and following the examples of Wolfe Tone, Robert Emmet and Edward Fitzgerald who were men of heroic mould. The need to revive the old heroic Ireland became most urgent, at least, Yeats and many of the Irish people felt it strongly in the last quarter of the nineteenth century when Ireland was united as a nation and forging ahead under the leadership of Isaac Butt and, later on, Charles Parnell.

Yeats was born in a period when Ireland was struggling hard to gain freedom and the leaders were using literature as a means to arouse patriotic feelings in the Irish people. The revolutionary Young Ireland Party consisted a number of poets who were politically active. The most notable among them were Thomas D'Arcy MacGee (1825-68), Sir Samuel Ferguson (1810-86), William Allingham (1824-89) and Thomas Osborne Davis (1814-45). When a nation struggles against the imperialist forces, the relation between the two becomes what Marx says the antagonism between the exploited and the exploiting classes. At this hour the entire nation is unified, except the lumpen elements, for its material and spiritual existence and looks back to its past, mythical or historical, which was glorious. Creative writers revive the old glory to awaken the spirit of their people. Yeats's predecessors—D'Arcy, Allingham, Ferguson and Davis —did revive Ireland's past glory and aroused nationalist feelings.

The impact of the current politics was great on the young poet. First, it made him a staunch nationalist who opposed the British rule all through his life. Secondly, it made him consider himself a link in the Irish poetic tradition. Although born in an Anglo-Irish family and taught English literature, he always considered himself an Irish poet writing in English. At the age of twenty-four he wrote to Elizabeth White:

> You will find it a good thing to make verses on Irish legends and places and so forth. It helps originality and makes one's verses sincere, and gives one less numerous competitors. Besides, one should love best what is nearest and most interwoven with one's life.[4]

The advice which he gave to Elizabeth was what he was actually following as a poet, that is, he was singing Ireland's glory to arouse nationalist feeling and reminding his people to revive the glorious past. He explored the ancient Irish mythology, rewrote the old heroic tales of the country and made aware his people of the present day misery. Later on, because of his bitter experiences in Irish politics he became a realist. The contradictions in society at different levels, Parnell's tragic death, opposition to the Irish Dramatic Movement, Synge's tragic death, controversy over *The Playboy of the Western World* and *Countess Cathleen,* and the Hugh Lane pictures, the Dublin Lockout, the Easter Rising, the Civil War and other political events changed his previous outlook and he wrote a different kind of poetry, still patriotic but universal in theme and exfoliated and terse in diction. Earlier he had a nascent view of the world but now it was mature and realistic.

"The Coming of Wisdom With Time" published in the volume *The Green Helmet and Other Poems* (1910) is a true expression of this change:

> Though leaves are many, the root is one;
> Through all the lying days of my youth
> I swayed my leaves and flowers in the sun;
> Now I may wither into the truth.[5] (*C.P.* 105)

My argument is that politics is a conscious effort of the ruling class to maintain its hold on the means of production and the struggle of the oppressed class to depose it and gain economic power. The main task of literature is to refine man's sensibility and liberate him from all kind of fetters. Like his fellow-poets Yeats, too, assumed the social responsibility. What was special in him was that he occasionally detached himself from the heat of action, pondered over the situation and systematised his stray thoughts. This systematisation of stray thoughts and calm meditation over the past, present and future of Ireland in particular and mankind in general gave his poetry an enduring quality and saved him from writing propagandist verse. His poetry is a fusion of the personal, the national and the universal.

Yeats was not Marx. But he had his humanity, a strong will to change the motley wearing Irish people into a heroic mould. In the pages that follow I have tried to explain how politics shaped Yeats's thought and poetry. I have discussed mainly the political poems and also those poems that were inspired by some political event but in the final form have a very faint trace or no trace at all. A great poet rises above the interests of his class and speaks for the entire humanity. Yeats always spoke for the entire nation and humanity.

REFERENCES

1. C.M. Bowra, *Poetry and Politics 1900-1960*, (London: CUP, 1966), 1.
2. *Ibid.*, 137.
3. W.B. Yeats, *Explorations*, (London: Macmillan, 1962), 457.
4. A. Wade, ed., *Letters of W.B. Yeats*, (Rupert Hart-Davis, 1959), 104.
5. *Collected Poems of W.B. Yeats*, (London: Macmillan, 1962), 105.

1

The Background

I

A poet should have a sense of history and a great poet more of it. Hippolyte-Taine's view that a creative work is the product of time, race and milieu is largely true, if we omit his mechanistic point of view. Yeats had a full sense of history. He studied Vico and Toynbee seriously and gave a mythical interpretation of the progress of civilization. Besides, he frequently referred to the pre-christian and post-christian Ireland. The ancient legendary figure Cuchulain occurs recurrently in his plays and poetry and to a large extent is his ideal. For him the eighteenth century was the golden period in the history of Ireland and Fitzgerald, Tone and Emmet were great heroic figures. For a fuller understanding of Yeats's poetry it is essential to know the Irish history, the contemporary political situation and his family background.

Of Ireland's pre-christian days little is known. There is a mixture of myth, legend and history. Cuchulain, Conchubar, Deirdre, Oisin, Emer and Fergus are partly legendary and partly historical. The known history of Ireland begins from the eighth century when the Norsemen invaded the northern part of country. The Gaelic people did not resist the invaders first as their High King ruled from Tara, near Dublin. But after sometime a long battle started. It lasted for about two hundred years when the High King Brian Boru won a decisive battle at Contarf in 1014. From that time the distinction between the Gael and the Gall (foreigners) was observed no longer. The Norsemen became native Irish in course of time.

After Brian Boru's death, Ireland was divided into small kingdoms. A defeated king Mac Murrough asked help from Henry II of England. Henry II found a great opportunity to rule Ireland. He sent Strongbow to help Mac Murrough; he after Mac Murrough's death became the King of Leinster. Slowly Ireland came under England's control which the Irish people never liked and continued to struggle for independence till 1921 when Ireland got autonomy.

The first person to unite Ireland into one nation was Hugh O'Neill. After initial success in war against England he was defeated. Although James I did not disinherit O'Neill nor punish him, he felt insecure and, in 1707, left the island for the Continent. His departure named "flight of earls" did not anger the Irish people; on the other hand they praised him and his comrades for leaving the country which had become alien for them. Brian Inglis comments:

> Although O'Neill was driven into his separatist ways by circumstances rather than by nationalist ideals, and although his defeat finally destroyed the old Ireland beyond hope of revival, he was to be one of the decisive influences in the moulding of nationalist tradition in later years.[1]

After O'Neill's departure King James systematically devised means to impose English language, laws and customs on the Irish people. Charles I continued the old policy. The Irish people resisted the English under the leadership of Owen Roe O'Neill who defeated General Monroe in a bloody battle but he too was crushed by the new ruler Oliver Cromwell. Cromwell abolished the Irish Parliament and his army tortured the patriots. Yeats has vented his feelings in the poem "The Curse of Cromwell":

> You ask what I have found, and far and wide I go:
> Nothing but Cromwell's house and Cromwell's
> murderous crew. (*C.P.* 350)

The great drawback of the risings against the British rule was the lack of organization; the entire country was divided into the Irish, Old English and New English population. Then there was religion to divide the people between the Catholics and the Protestants. The racial differences and religious groups thwarted the process of unity. During the reign of William III and Queen

Anne, the total aim of the English government was to keep Ireland dependent on England commercially and politically, the policy that was adopted later on for India. This policy to drain wealth from Ireland to England was first resisted by Jonathan Swift who advised in *The Drapier Letters* to burn everything English but their coal.

After some time the Patriot party was founded under the leadership of Henry Grattan and the Earl of Charlemont who, at first devoted their energy to secure commercial parity with England but, soon, realized that without political freedom, economic exploitation would not be stopped. The Duke of Leinster and the Earl of Charlemont organized military to win freedom through revolution. Henry Grattan was made the party's parliamentary spokesman to obtain a new constitution. However, a tactical blunder of Grattan frustrated the entire movement.

After Grattan's failure, the leadership was taken over by Wolfe Tone. Grattan had wanted to revise the 1782 constitution but Tone asserted that the constitution had "only enabled Irishmen to sell at a much higher price their honour, their integrity, and the interests of their country."[2]

The English government saw a greater danger in Tone than in Grattan. Tone was implicated in a conspiracy case and the charge of treason was levelled against him. In the meantime Arthur O' Connor and Lord Edward Fitzgerald planned rebellion. But before they could execute it, the English government got scent of it. They were rounded up. Fitzgerald was mortally wounded; even Tone who had initial success was defeated and captured. He committed suicide while in jail.

The great success of Tone and Fitzgerald was that they united Ireland into a nation. Yeats remembered these leaders of the United Irishmen in the poem "September 1913." Contrasting the attitude of the anti-Parnellites with that of the United Irishmen he asked:

> Was it...
>
> For this Edward Fitzgerald died
> And Robert Emmet and Wolfe Tone
> All that delirium of the brave? (*C.P.* 121)

Only after five years of Tone's rising, Robert Emmet led another rising in 1803. But he too was defeated. Then followed a different strategy under the leadership of David O'Connell, a barrister of repute, who exposed the sinister design of the English government behind every law. He struggled for full autonomy. He was ably supported by Thomas Davis, John Blake Dillon and Charles Gavan Duffy. After Davis's death the mantle fell on Smith O'Brien and John Mitchel. They led another uprising but were defeated and arrested. At first they were given death sentences but later on the sentences were converted into life-imprisonment and deportation.

The Great Famine stopped all political activities. A sizeable number of people migrated to America for job. Even after the famine, emigration to America continued but the process of emigration had a telling effect upon the emigrants. Continued starvation, hazardous journey in ships and exploitation by the American planters and general hostility of the native people made them angry.* Keenly aware of the injustice they suffered, they always thought of Ireland and her independence. As they had earlier fought for the Repeal and the fire of nationalism was still alive in their heart, they formed a group called the Fenians to support the cause of Ireland. Soon Fenianism spread from America to Ireland and England.

John O'Leary was the leader of the Fenian group in Ireland. He planned an uprising but bad organization and leakage of secrets damaged everything. O'Leary was deported to France and was allowed to return towards the fag end of life. W.B. Yeats joined his group and became a Fenian.

II

The small size and the long struggle for freedom made every Irishman a nationalist. Yeats had the extra privilege as his father was a friend of Isaac Butt who became Ireland's leader after

* Karl Marx wrote: "The Irish chased from their native soil by the bulls and the sheep, reassemble in North America where they constitute a huge, ever-growing section of the population. Their only thought, their only passion is hatred for England." *Selected Works* Vol. II (Moscow: Progress Publishers, 1969), 176.

O'Leary's fall. He was born at a time when Ireland was politically charged and people worshipped the past heroes. During his childhood the Fenian movement was at its peak and a little later Isaac Butt and Charles Parnell dominated the scene. All the three: John O'Leary, Isaac Butt and Charles Parnell were full of praise for the Young Irelanders who had aroused nationalist feelings by means of their literary works. Yeats read in his youth the works of Davis, Allingham, Ferguson and Standish O'Grady with great interest. In 1891, when he had become an important poet of Ireland, he tried to convince his people of the talents of Ferguson and Standish O'Grady. He recollected his efforts in *Autobiographies*:

> In 1891 I had founded in London the Irish literary society, joined by most London journalists of Irish birth, couple of years later in Dublin, the National Literary Society; these societies had given, as I intended, opportunity to a new generation of critics and writers to denounce the propagandist verse and prose that had gone by the name of Irish literature, and to substitute for it certain neglected writers: Sir Samuel Ferguson, a writer of ballads in their eighteenth century sincerity; Standish O'Grady, whose *History of Ireland* retold the Irish heroic tales in romantic Carlylean prose; the Clarence Mangan of the *Dark Rosaleen* and *O'Hussey's Ode to the Maguire,* our one poet raised to the first rank by intensity, and only that in these or perhaps in the second of these poems.[3]

In his two articles titled "The Poetry of Sir Samuel Ferguson," the first published in the *Irish Fiveside* of October 9, 1886 and the second in *Dublin University Review* of November 1886, he praised Ferguson that he had shown the other poets the path to the treasure of the rich Irish legends. Classifying legends into seven cycles—the Indian, the Homeric, the Charlemagnic, the Arthurian, the Scandinavian and the Irish—he commented:

> Sir Samuel Ferguson's special claim to our attention is that he went back to the Irish cycle, finding it, in truth, a fountain that in the passage of centuries, was overgrown with weeds and grass, so that the very way to it was forgotten of the poets;....[4]

In the same article he criticized Professor Dowden for his preference to English literature and indifference to Irish literature.

Yeats, as said earlier, came in contact with Fenianism when John O'Leary after his long exile in France returned to Ireland in 1885. He met him for the first time at the Contemporary Club. He found in O'Leary the man of his ideal, a man who was a true successor of Wolfe Tone and Thomas Davis. Although the armed uprising failed miserably, the impact of O'Leary, Stephens and Luby was lasting and the younger generation followed their ideals and methods till Ireland became independent. Terence de Vere White writes in *Modern Ireland*:

> Though Fenianism seemed to have failed, the spirit of the movement was to remain alive and have lasting consequences. Many of its supporters were labourers in the country and Irish-minded people in the towns who wanted to fight for Ireland.
>
> As a result of the Fenian revolts, there were a great many state prisoners, and the Protestant Barrister Isaac Butt became a new national leader because of his efforts for their release.[5]

No doubt, after his return from France O'Leary was surrounded by young men. Yeats under his influence joined the Fenian Brotherhood. Patrick McCartan, a Fenian, writes:

> More than once I heard on this side of the Atlantic that John O'Leary, when head of the Fenians, had sworn Yeats into the organization. During his visit to this country [America] in 1933 I asked Yeats if this were true. He said he never took any oath but regarded himself as one of the party.[6]

Even if Yeats did not take oath he remained a Fenian at heart. It was from O'Leary that he learnt about Thomas Davis in detail. How much he was influenced by the Fenian leader can be easily guessed if we read his autobiography. He acknowledges his indebtedness to O'Leary in glowing words:

> From these debates, from O'Leary's conversation and from the Irish books he lent or gave me has come all I have set my hand to since.[7]

Later on, Leary became a symbol of all that was noble and heroic for Yeats. Deeply grieved at the unheroic attitude of his countrymen he wrote in "September 1913":

> Romantic Ireland's dead and gone
> It's with O'Leary in the grave.

In fact, O'Leary gave him more than he has acknowledged in *Autobiographies.* Perhaps, Yeats was so much with O'Leary that he did not think it necessary to write an essay on his indebtedness to him. Frank O'Connor has very clearly written about the Fenian leader's influence on him:

> Yet, but for an accidental meeting with the old Fenian leader John O'Leary Yeats might easily have ended as a fine minor poet like Walter De la Mare. 1886 was a turning point in life because under O'Leary's influence he began to use Irish material in the way of Ferguson and Mangan, and after that he was dealing with a situation so explosive that he could not afford to trifle with it. He might be persecuted; he might even go in danger of his life; but he was always to be in the thick of things.[8]

Frank O'Connor's comment supports my view that Yeats's involvement in Irish politics gave substance to his poetry; without awareness of Irish history and the Irish literary tradition he would have remained imprisoned in the world of Arcady.

As described earlier, the Home Rule League founded by Isaac Butt in 1858 began to gain popularity after O'Leary's exile. Before joining the Fenian Brotherhood, Yeats had attended a branch of the Home Rule League. Isaac Butt's demand was an Irish Parliament elected by the people of Ireland to look after their welfare. Although it was a very moderate demand the English government declined it. After some time, the leadership was taken over by the other political party, Land League, led by Michael Davitt on the line of Mitchel and Lalor. Yeats liked the Land League party and maintained a good relationship with Davitt. The following letter written to Yeats reveals the poet's feelings for the Land League and Michael Davitt:

Dalkey, Co. Dublin
4 Nov. 1899

My dear Mr. Yeats,

It is indeed most kind of you to think of writing so complimentary a letter.

I spoke, just as I felt, in my last utterance in the H. of Commons, in the full conviction that I would serve the cause of Irish liberty best with right-thinking minds everywhere by spurning a craven expediency and basing Ireland's right & claim to freedom upon the Justice and Right which we should advocate for every people defending their independence.

I am glad I got out of Parliament on those lines. If you will read my speech at Aughamore tomorrow (in Monday's Freeman) you will see that there were good reasons why I was resolved to regain my freedom from Party restraints.

What a magnificent struggle the Boers are making! And we—are 25,000,000 of Celts in the world population!—The Boers are 1,50,000!!

With kind regards.

Yours truly
MICHAEL DAVITT

Although Yeats continued his relations with Davitt he took more interest in the activities of the Home Rule League. Charles Parnell, the new leader became his hero. Parnell united all the separatist elements into Ireland and, as a leader in the Parliament, exposed all the designs of the government and pleaded for concessions that could give autonomy to the nation. Parnell's fall shocked Yeats and he defended the dejected and fallen leader's case in two articles and always counted him as one of the heroes of Ireland. In addition, he wrote two poems on Parnell and made him a symbol of all that is noble, heroic and tragic in his important poems.

III

External influences are important, no doubt; but family background is more important. The seed of nationalism germinated in Yeats's boyhood. Yeats involved himself in the Irish politics because he was conditioned as a nationalist at home. The family tradition, the close relatives, the friend circle and his own experiences as a child and a boy made him firmly rooted in Ireland's soil. His early life shows why and how he became a staunch nationalist and why his views on the identity of the individual, the relationship between the individual and society and the church and the state differed so radically from the conventional ideas held superstitiously by the Irish people.

Yeats was born in a Protestant Anglo-Irish family. We have already seen that almost all the national heroes right from O'Connell and Grattan were Protestant Anglo-Irish and it was natural for his parents to nourish Irish nationalism and be proud of the lineage. Among the ancestors of Yeats there was one Benjamin Yeats a member of the mercantile community which had accepted Dean Swift as its leader and struck the first note of the Irish Protestant nationalism. Rev. William Butler Yeats, poet's grandfather was a friend of Isaac Butt and, with him, edited Dublin University Magazine. Yeats learnt much about him and Isaac Butt from his conversation with his father. At his mother's home, he developed love for the countryside and fairy tales that dominate his early poetry. His grandfather (motherside) William Pollexfen was a kind and generous man who, like John O'Leary, avoided self-propaganda and never told anyone, even his wife, how bravely he fought and won freedom of a Spanish city.[9] Yeats narrates one more incident of his fortitude:

> He had great physical strength and had the reputation of never ordering a man to do anything he would not do himself. He owned many sailing ships and once when a captain just come to anchor at Rosses Point reported something wrong with the rudder, had sent a messenger to say, 'Send a man down yourself,' and not being obeyed, he dived from the main deck, all the neighbourhood lined along the pebbles of the shore. He came up with his skin torn but well informed about the rudder.[10]

William Pollexfen always kept a hatchet at his bedside for the burglars. Yeats was so much impressed by him that he confused between the images of God and his grandfather. Yet Pollexfen never inspired awe in him; he was a very gentle and affectionate old man. It was he who made the timid and physically frail Yeats grow into a courageous boy, bold enough to fight against the bully Cyril Vosey at Godolphin School and go at night to bring a railway pass from Rosses Point. For mature Yeats Pollexfen became the epitome of heroic qualities:

> Even today when I read *King Lear* his image is always before me, and I often wonder if the delight in passionate men in my plays and in my poetry is more than his memory.[11]

His life at Sligo was pleasant and happy; the members of the Pollexfen family were kind and sympathetic to him and if he remembered his "childhood but its pain" it was because of his own physical weakness that made him feel inferior to the children of the family. At Sligo he came in contact with the Middletons, partner and relative of the Pollexfens, from whom he learnt a number of ghost stories which he wrote in his youth and published with certain revisions in the Irish magazines. Later on, he collected those published stories and published them under the title *Celtic Twilight.* Between Sligo and Rosses Point there was the house of Mary, Yeats's great aunt, on the top of a hill. She was full of family history. Yeats narrates in *Autobiographies* the details of her character and says that he learnt from her that the Yeats family had been respectable and that Dean Swift and Oliver Goldsmith were friends of his ancestors.[12] The memory of Sligo was always sweet for him. When he was in London he remembered the place and the people with poignant feelings. He writes in *Autobiographies*:

> Years afterwards, when I was ten or twelve years old and in London, I would remember Sligo with tears, and when I began to write, it was there, I hoped to find my audience.[13]

The bitter experiences in London accentuated his love of Ireland and her people further. His life in London was rather miserable; young Yeats, his brothers and sisters always longed for home. J.B. Yeats, inspite of his great talent was not financially successful and, so, Yeats was admitted to Godolphin, a school where students from the low income group of the professional class studied. The atmosphere though congenial to the taste of young Yeats aroused in him hatred for England; the derision of Ireland and the Irish people was too much for him. He had to fight sometimes with the English boys. He narrates in *Autobiographies* that one day some boys surrounded him and asked his father's name, profession and income. Before he could say anything, a boy passed an insulting remark. Unable to tolerate humiliation Yeats replied sharply. The result was that he had to fight with the entire group. Fights of this type continued as long he was in school. Here he came to realize that the Irish and the English were two nations and they could never be united; the seed of nationalism which was sown in his early childhood germinated in Godolphin but watered by hatred. He was a poor boxer and his friend, an athlete, always defeated him. Later on, he learnt how to box but he never got better of him. But one day when he heard the words "mad Irishman" he boxed well out of rage. He describes the incident in *Autobiographies*:

> One day his [the athlete friend's] father, an elderly banker, brought us out into the garden and tried to make box in a cold-blooded courteous way, but it was no use. At last he said I might go near the boys again and I was no sooner inside the gate of the playing field than a boy flung a handful of mud and cried out, "Mad Irishman." I hit him several times on the face without being hit, till the boys round said we should make friends.[14]

The small plant of hatred against England as a nation grew into a large tree in course of time and he never spared the English people or the Crown whenever he got opportunity, Lady Dorothy Wellesley narrates an account of his attack on the king of England:

> He seemed exhausted on arrival here at 5 O'clock. After tea (which he neither ate nor drank) he read me a new poem about which he had previously written, opening thus: 'you won't like this because it attacks King George V.' 'But I don't care two hoots about George V,' I replied angrily realizing that this was his first inevitable attack upon the English which must continue for many days. I listened while he read his poem.[15]

Like Swift he could love individual English men but hated the British empire:

> Out of Ireland have we come
> Great hatred little room
> Maimed us at the start,
> I carry from my mother's womb
> A fanatic heart.

At Godolphin the English boys talked of Agincourt, Calais and Cressey but he thought of the ancient heroes of Ireland and the beautiful landscape of Sligo. The happiest moments in his boyhood in London were the sweet memories of Sligo, people there, the lush green forests, the blue hills, the lapping lakes and the evening fairy-tales. Sometimes he was so overwhelmed with nostalgic memories that he wept sadly:

> A poignant memory came upon me the other day while I was passing the drinking fountain near Holland Park, for there I and my sister had spoken together of our longing for Sligo and our hatred of London. I know we were both very close to tears and remember with wonder, for I had never known anyone that cared for such mementoes, that I longed for a sod of earth from some field I knew, something of Sligo to hold in my hand.[16]

He remained indifferent to the victories won by the English at Cressey and Agincourt and cared little for the Union Jack of which the English boys were proud. He prided himself on the Land League, the Irish heroes and his grandfather, Pollexfen.

The last, perhaps the most significant, influence to shape his thought and poetry was that of the Irish nationalist poets and prose-writers, chiefly Thomas Davis, Clarence Mangan, Samuel Ferguson, William Allingham, Standish O'Grady and Dr. Douglas Hyde. Yeats read these writers seriously, reviewed them in different magazines and praised them for their sincerity of feeling and fire of nationalism. For him Mangan, Ferguson, Davis and Allingham were the supreme Irish poets comparable to many in England. He admired Ferguson for his deft handling of Irish materials, Davis for writing political poems, Mangan for sincerity of feeling Allingham for Irishry, Carleton and Standish

O'Grady* for reviving the glorious past of Ireland, and criticized Professor Dowden for remaining indifferent to these Irish writers.**

Yeats, however, was cautious in his appraisal of the nationalist poets and always made distinction between genuine poetry and propagandist verse. His father was not only a barrister but also a very good painter and connoisseur of literature. Jack Yeats recited important works of English poetry before the son, explained the reason for his preference to certain poets and allowed the young poet to discuss poetry and politics with him.***

These diverse influences—the long struggle for freedom and the sacrifice of the past heroes, the contemporary political situation, the family background, the unhappy life in London and the nationalist literature—made Yeats a strong nationalist, a hero worshipper, firmly rooted in the soil of his country and a poet for whom poetry and politics were compounded into one. He sincerely felt that Ireland had to be a free nation for the achievement of Unity of Culture and Unity of Being.

---

* Yeats wrote three articles on Ferguson, two on Allingham, two on Clarence Mangan, three on Carleton, and the article titled "Popular Ballad Poetry of Ireland" which surveys all the important Irish poets and, a little later, a series of articles under the general title "Irish National Literature."

** Yeats criticized Professor Dowden in the article "Professor Dowden and Irish Literature."

All the essays and articles are available in R. Frayne. (ed.) *The Uncollected Prose* Vol. I & II (London: Macmillan, 1971).

*** A.N. Jeffares quotes Elizabeth's diary in his article "John Butler Yeats":

"Elizabeth's diary entry for 9 September 1888, when W.B. Yeats was twenty-three—

> "I can hear a murmur of talk from the dining-room where Papa and Willie are arguing something or other. Sometimes they raise their voices so high that a stranger might fancy that they were both in a rage, not at all, it is only their way of arguing because they are the natives of the Emerald Isle."

A.N. Jeffares and K.G.W. Cross ed., *In Excited Reverie* (London: Macmillan, 1965), 40.

REFERENCES

1. Brian Inglis, *The Story of Ireland*, (London: Faber and Faber, 1956), 51.
2. *Ibid.*, 68.
3. W.B. Yeats, *Autobiographies*, (London: Macmillan, 1956), 395-96.
4. John P. Frayne, ed., *Uncollected Prose of W.B. Yeats*, Vol. I (London: Macmillan, 1970), 82.
5. Terence de Vere White, *Modern Ireland*, (London: Faber and Faber, 1960), 43.
6. John Unterecker (ed.), *Yeats and Patrick McCarton: A Fenian Friendship*, (Dublin: Dolmen Press, 1965), 428-29.
7. W.B. Yeats, *Autobiographies*, 101.
8. Frank O'Connor, *The Backward Look*, (London: Macmillan, 1965), 165.
9. W.B. Yeats, *Autobiographies*, 6.
10. *Ibid.*, 7.
11. *Ibid.*, 9.
12. *Ibid.*, 22.
13. *Ibid.*, 18.
14. *Ibid.*, 37.
15. *Letters on Poetry from W.B. Yeats to Lady Dorothy Wellesley*, (London: OUP, 1940), 171.
16. W.B. Yeats, *Autobiographies*, 31.

2

THE CELTIC TWILIGHT

1

Yeats's early poetry, the poetry he wrote before he came in contact with O'Leary and the nationalist poets, is in the tradition of the English romantic poets, especially of the early Spenser and the early Shelley. Yeats's temptation to follow the English romantic poets was due to the reason that he was brought up in that tradition and he found no other opening in the start of his poetical career.* Poems like "*The Song of the Fairies*" and "*The Boat, the Cloak and the Shoes*" (the first title "*The Voices*") are the product of a poet who is suffering from some vaguely known cause. Melancholy is the dominant strain in these poems:

What do you make so fair and bright?

I make the cloak of sorrow:
O lovely to see in all men's sight
Shall be the cloak of Sorrow
In all men's sight.

("The Boat, the Cloak and the Shoes," *C.P.* 10)

In the same vein are the poems "Miserrimus," renamed "The Song of the Happy Shepherd, and "The Song of the Last Arcadia" renamed "The Sad Shepherd" which owe largely to Spenser for style and to Shelley for vocabulary. Here Yeats is more inclined to the truth of dreams and words:

But O sick children of the world
Of all the many changing things

* "I had begun to write poetry in imitation of Shelley and Edmund Spenser, play after play—for my father exalted dramatic poetry above all other kinds—and I invented fantastic and incoherent plots." *Autobiographies*, 66.

In dreary dancing past us whirled
To the cracked tune that Chronos sings
Words alone are certain good.

And,

But ah! she dreams not now; dream thou
For fair are poppies on the brow
Dream, dream, for this is also sooth.

("The Song of the Happy Shepherd," *C.P.* 7-8)

Likewise there is the same feeling of languor and melancholy in "The Sad Shepherd":

I will my heavy story tell
Till my own words, echoing, re-echoing, shall send
Their sadness through a hollow, pearly heart
And my own tale again for me shall sing;
And my own whispering words be comforting
And lo! my ancient burden may depart.

But it does not happen:

Then he sang softly nigh the pearly rim
But the sad dweller by the sea-ways lone
Changed all he sang to inarticulate moan
Among all her wildering whirls, forgetting him.

(*C.P.* 9)

The world of these poems is basically Arcadian, a world where thin, emaciated, pale lovers pine for what is not and sing songs of faint emotions and the sad world. They are the conventional romantic lovers who need someone to wake them to the world of prosaic reality. The other poems written before 1889 are of the same tenor, marked by languor, heaviness, indolence and melancholy; they are the expression of a pale dreamy youth living in a world of fantasy far away from our world of heat and dust. Naturally, these poems, inspite of their melody and perfection of technique, ring a hollow note.

Although "Anashuya and Vijaya" is written under the influence of Babu Mohini Chatterjee and deals with the theme of two selves and the relation between soul and body, it fails as a philosophical poem. The second Indian poem "The Indian to

His Love" is equally hazy and vague. The only remarkable lines in it are: "A parrot sways upon a tree/Raging at his image in the enamelled sea." The third Indian poem is certainly a good mystic poem which describes God's manifestation in different forms.

After comparing Yeats's poetry with that of the minor romantics and the pre-Raphaelites F.R. Leavis concluded that there was little difference between the two. But his conclusion is based upon incomplete data, that is, he studied the poems written before 1889.

For writing a very inferior kind of poetry tinged with languor and melancholy, we need not be harsh to young Yeats. While learning his trade he functioned like a *bricoleur* who creates a new structure by dismantling the old structure. The novice Yeats was not able to give new meaning to the existing words nor make meaningful experiments with syntax. For writing poetry substantial and sinewy, he needed experiences of life which would provide solidity and hardness.

It was his active participation in politics and study of Irish history and literature that enabled him to choose the right path which led him to the desired goal.* The efforts of the Irish patriots to awaken the Irish people by singing the glory of ancient Ireland made a great impact on the young poet who was not satisfied with the kind of poetry he was writing. In the poetry of Davis, Allingham, Mangan and Standish O'Grady he found a rich treasure. Now, his first aim was to revive Ireland culturally and bring it to the level of England. In his opinion, Ireland was definitely militant and fierce but this was the characteristic of the barbarians also; the civilized and the cultured had to be tender and loving. He begins his article "Popular Ballad Poetry of Ireland," written in 1887 but published in 1889, with the following words:

---

* "The debates," writes A.N. Jeffares, "in the Young Ireland Society, O'Leary's conversation, and the patriotic books he read at the period were the main reasons for his subsequent work." *W.B. Yeats: Man and the Poet*, 35.

For a detailed discussion on the partnership between O'Leary and Yeats, see Richard Fallis, *The Irish Renaissance*, 3-6.

> Behind Ireland, fierce and militant, is Ireland poetic passionate, remembering, idyllic, fanciful and always patriotic. With this second Ireland only I have to do in this article....[1]

In this article, he discusses only those poets who wrote faithfully about the Irish people and omitted Moore, Lever and Lover on the ground that "Moore lived in the drawing rooms" and "Lever and Lover, kept apart by opinion from the body of the nation, wrote ever with one eye on London."[2] He praises his favourite writers for their sincerity and directness of style.

> Other poets have found refuge from their unhappiness in philosophical subtleties and aerial turnings and pirouettings of the spirit. But this man, Mangan, born in a torpid city, could only write in diverse fashions. 'I am miserable.' No hopes! No philosophy! No illusions! A brute cry from the gutters of the earth! and for solace or rather for a drug—this—

> No more, no more with aching brow,
>   And restless heart, and burning brain
> We ask the When and Where, the How
>   And ask in vain.
>
> And all philosophy, all faith,
>   All earthly—all celestial lore
> Have but one Voice, which only saith—
>   Endure—adore.[3]

Yeats's review of Mangan and the other nationalist poets made the Irish people aware of the richness of their own literature and think seriously how long they would go on studying English literature, a literature of the foreign soil. The younger generation of poets began to realize that the true source of their poetry was Ireland and her people and there was no use going to Milton, Pope and Wordsworth. It was also that after reading Mangan Yeats realized his own weakness and began to denounce passive suffering. He abandoned the falsely learnt Keatsian concept of beauty and truth. Later on he reminisced his false idea of poetry and art he had held in the beginning of his poetical career:

> In my heart I thought that only beautiful things should be painted and that only beautiful things and stuff of dreams were beautiful. And I almost quarrelled with my father

> when he made a large water-colour, one of his finest pictures and now lost, of a consumptive beggar.[4]

This change in Yeats's attitude and his coming to terms with reality is discernible in poems like "The Madness of King Goll," "The Lost Child," "Down by the Salley Gardens," "The Ballad of Father O'Hart," "The Meditation of the Old Fisherman," "The Ballad of Moll Magee," and "The Ballad of the Foxhunter." These ballads based on the old Gaelic poems or the stories he had heard at Sligo and home are rooted in the soil of Ireland and mark his break with the world of Arcady. Professor John Unterecker points out:

> If the first eight poems of *Crossways,* Indian and Arcadian in subject-matter, represent one road. Yeats briefly wandered on, the remaining eight grimly Irish, represent the one he finally travelled.[5]

Yeats took the right decision to abandon the alien path he had early taken; if he had stayed in the remote world of Arcady or the Indian world of his fantasy for a long time he would have achieved the distinction of a minor romantic poet, but not a great modern poet as we know him today. It was his happy return to the hard soil of the contemporary Ireland that made his poetry substantial. The eight "Irish" poems in *Crossways,* though based on old stories, are marked by Yeats's originality. They, of course, as pointed out by David Daiches,[6] present the dichotomy between the human world and the wild world, but what is more important is that they depict the problems of the common Irish people and their beliefs and real feelings.

"The Madness of King Goll" depicts the circumstances under which King Goll, who once ruled from Ith to Emain and commanded even the animal world, went out of mind. He tells of his past in the first three stanzas that he was a powerful ruler whom poets praised in hyperboles. Every stanza ends with the refrain "They will not hush, the leaves a-flutter round me, the beech leaves old." The next three stanza describe his life of madness. In course of his wanderings he happens to reach a town late at night. Unable to make any contact with the towns-people, he wanders aimlessly till he finds a tympan. Taking it away to the woods, he sings of "some inhuman misery" but soon finds that the wires are broken. He, therefore, has to wander without the musical instrument:

> I must wander wood and hill
> Through summer's heat and winter's cold.

According to David Daiches, the tragedy of King Goll is his failure to make contact with the domestic life. His departure from the domestic life to the wild nature is suggested by juxtaposition of contrasting images—"cushioned" and "otter-skin," "fields" and "bubbling mire" and "keen eyes of men" and "keen stars." Daiches is right in his interpretation. But it is also that Yeats in the first version was more concerned with telling the stories of legendary figures in verse:

"The Stolen Child" is a poetic representation of the popular belief that fairies sometimes lure human beings to their land, the land of heart's desire. Their world is marked by jollity and gaiety of which the human world has little trace:

> To and fro we leap
> And chase the frothy bubbles
> While the world is full of troubles
> And is anxious in its sleep. (*C.P.* 20)

The child who has little understanding of the real world is enticed to the fairy world of which he has no knowledge. The fairies are happy at the success of their trick:

> Away with us he's going
> The solemn-eyed:
> He'll hear no more the lowing
> Of the calves on the warm hillside
> Or the Kettle on the hob
> Sing peace into his breast,
> Or see the brown mice bob
> Round and round the oatmeal chest. (*C.P.* 21)

Professor A.N. Jeffares comments:

> This poem ['The Stolen Child'] marks the shift from Arcadian and Indian scenes to Irish—Yeats wrote later that for such reasons as those in 'Ireland and the arts' (E & I 203) he convinced himself that he should never 'go for the scenery of a poem to any country but my own, and I think that I shall hold to that conviction to the end.'[7]

We cannot but agree with this view; the places mentioned are in the Sligo area. Sleuth Wood lies between Lough Gill and Dromahair, Rosses is between Knocknarea and Ben Bulben and both these places were believed to be haunted by fairies in Yeats's time and if anyone slept at these places at night his or her soul would be carried by fairies.

However, the poem is partly realistic, Yeats wrote in his letter dated 14 March 1888 to Katharine Tynan that in the process of correcting his poems he had noticed things about his poetry he had not known before:

> It was almost all a flight into fairyland from the real world.... The Chorus to the 'Stolen Child' sums it up—that it is not the poetry of insight and knowledge but of longing and complaint—the cry of the heart and necessity. I hope that some day to alter that and write poetry of insight and knowledge.[8]

"Down by the Salley Gardens" is modelled on an old song. Yeats explains in the footnote to the poem that it is "an attempt to reconstruct an old peasant woman in the village of Ballysodare, Sligo who, often sings them to herself."[9]

Jeffares in his *Commentary* refers to H.C. Shield's article "Yeats and the Salley Gardens" published in the journal *Hermethena* (Autumn 1965). H.E. Shield in that article has compared both the old ballad and Yeats's poem and showed the close similarities between them, particularly the second and the third stanzas.

Although "Down by the Salley Gardens" is an adaptation, Yeats's originality cannot be doubted; whereas the old ballad is a simple denunciation of the corrupt ways of money—"Gold is the root of evil although it wears a glittering hue/causes many a lad and lass to part through their hearts like mine be e'er so true;" Yeats's poem presents a contrast between innocence and experience—"She bid me take life easy as the grass grows on weirs/But I was young and foolish and now am full of tears."

Disillusionment, after bitter experience, is again the theme of "The Meditation of the Old Fisherman." The refrain "When I was a boy with never a crack in heart" occurring regularly at the end of each stanza shows the contrast between the happy past and the sad present.

Both "Down by the Salley Gardens" and "The Meditation of the Old Fisherman" anticipate the later Yeats. The contrast between the innocent youth and the experienced man is presented in a simplified way; the antinomy of youth and age is presented in a much more complex way in the later poems.

The next poem "The Ballad of the Foxhunter" is more than the story of an old foxhunter's death; it stresses the dichotomy of domesticity and wilderness, with preference for the domestic life. The dying Foxhunter, surrounded by his family members, asks Rody, the huntsman, to blow his horn to receive a reply from the hills (an image of the wild nature) if they are sympathetic to him. The negative reply surprises him. He asks Rody again to blow the horn but this time the huntsman refuses to do so because it is a sheer foolishness to expect sympathy from the wild. In contrast to the apathy of wilderness is the warmth of domesticity, symbolized by men and hounds. The blind hound, the foxhunter's old companion, is in perfect communion with him:

> The blind hound with a mournful head;
> Lifts slow his wintry head;
> The servants bear the body in
> The hounds wail for the dead. (*C.P.* 29)

Between "The Ballad of Moll Magee" and "The Ballad of Father O'Hart," the latter is more realistic, "Moll Magee" is a simple narration of a poor deserted women who has lost her only child and, unable to bear the shock and injustice of her husband, she has gone mad. Yeats's depiction of the poor Irish woman is realistic and moving at the same time. What marks the sublimity of the poem is the simple neutral narration of the unusual suffering of the plain-hearted Moll Magee and her faith in God that he will take notice of her plight some day and save her:

> And sometimes I am sure she knows
> When, openin' wide His door,
> God lights the stars, His candles
> And looks upon the poor. (*C.P.* 27)

This stanza and the concluding stanza have ambiguous construction. Here the poet identifies himself with Moll Magee by adding—"I am sure" in this stanza and omitting the quotation marks in the final stanza, a technique later on adopted and mastered by Sylvia Plath, especially in the poem "The Cut."

> So now, ye little childer
> Ye won't fling stones at me;
> But gather with your shining looks
> And pity Moll Magee. (*C.P.* 27)

"The Ballad of Father O'Hart,"which sings the life of the good clergyman, is important in many ways. The Father is certainly a traditional figure but what is appealing in the poem is the realistic description of his poverty:

> And he wore small holes in his shoes
> And he wore large holes in his gown. (*C.P.* 24)

But unmindful of the betrayal of the upstarts who usurped his land, he went on to serve his parishioners. His greatest contribution to the people of the land was abolition of the keening system, a custom which allowed the professionals to mourn the dead. The great reward of his campaign against professional mourning was that when he died at the age of ninety-four, the well-wishers only lamented his death.

These eight poems rooted in the Irish soil are better than the poems he had written earlier. He realized this fact well in time. He wrote to Katharine Tynan:

> I feel more and more that we shall have a school of poetry founded on Irish myth and history—a neo-romantic movement.[10]

The second important feature of these poems is that they depict the common people's life. However, he does not romanticise them; he is aware of their problems and critical of the exploiters. Certainly, the influence of Davis and Mangan is evident. Here he is like William Blake who criticised the evils prevalent in society and expressed sympathy for the poor.

After these short poems, Yeats wrote the ambitious *Wanderings of Oisin* that won him immediate fame. Based on the legend of the Fenian hero, Oisin, this poem narrates his adventures and love with Niamh, a Danaan; and return to Ireland after three hundred years. "The events it describes," writes Yeats, "like most of the poems in this volume (*Wanderings of Oisin and Other Poems*) are supposed to have taken place rather in the indefinite period, made up of many periods, described by the folk-tales, than in any particular century; it, therefore, like the other Fenian stories themselves mixes much that is medieval with much that is ancient. The Gaelic poems do not make Oisin go to more than one island, but a story in *Silva Gadelica* describes 'four paradises,' an island to the north, an island to the south, an island to the west and Adam's paradise in the east."[11]

The poem opens with the conversation between St. Patrick and Oisin who is "bent, and bald, and blind?" Oisin tells the story of his adventures how he met Niamh, fell in love with her and travelled with her to three islands for three centuries and, later, come to Ireland for the love of his people. In the first part he describes his meeting with Niamh, daughter of Aengus and Edain, her expression of love and his marriage with her in the island of fairies. The second part narrates his fierce fight with the protean demon and his spectacular victory:

> And then I drew the livid chop
> Of a drowned dripping body to my breast
> Horror from horror grew; but when the west
> Had surged up in a plumy fire, I drave
> Through heart and spine; and cast him in the wave
> Lest Niamh shudder." (*C.P.* 428-29)

Living with Niamh for three hundred years, he remembers his countrymen, the Fenians, and wishes to see them:

> O Niamh! O white one! if only a twelve hour day,
> I must gaze on the beard of Finn, and move where
> the old men and young
>
> In the Fenians' dwellings of wattle lean on
> chessboards and play
> Ah sweet to me now were even bald Conan's
> slanderous tongue. (*C.P.* 446)

Niamh allows him to visit his country but warns him of the danger of touching the ground. Returning home, he finds it a changed country. The Fenians are there no more as rulers of Ireland and what is worse is that the Irish people are reduced to abject poverty and have to toil hard to earn their bread. He sees two of his countrymen carrying a sack of sand and falling down under the pressure of the heavy weight. Oisin is deeply distressed at the pathetic sight and overpowered by the feeling of pity he jumps off his horse to lift the emaciated bodies. But the touch of the ground breaks the spell that made him immortal and ever young; he becomes a stooping old man instantly: "A creeping old man full of sleep, with the spittle on his beard never dry."

Wanderings of Oisin is the result of Yeats's active involvement in Irish politics and study of the contemporary patriotic literature. The great quality of the poem is that, though modelled partly on Spenser's *Fairy Queen* it is rooted in the Irish soil. In the words of R. Fallis, it "is a fine example of Ferguson's technique of dealing with Irish legend, in this case the Fenian stories, coupled to [sic] Yeats's sensibility."[12] But the total effect of the poem is more than this; there is the fusion of politics and aesthetics both. The logical structure is the series of adventures of the Fenian, patterned on the old poems of knight-errantry. But the irrelevant local texture changes it into a work of art; the images, the diction and the narrative technique make a highly emotional appeal to us. The fight between Oisin and the demon is actually an imagined fight between the Fenians of the nineteenth century and the British empire. Ellmann interprets it:

> Then he makes a second voyage to a different kind of island, where 'rose a world of tower/And blackness in the dark.' Surely this is a symbolical England seen through Irish eyes. Here is the castle of Manannan, the old God of the sea, his place taken now by a 'brown demon.' The demon has enchained a beautiful lady who, like the enchained young man in 'The Two Titans,' symbolises Ireland.[13]

Oisin's wish to see the Fenians, his anguish at the poor conditions of the Irish people and his determination to revive the old glory, all indicate to the fact that Yeats has a political purpose in writing this poem. Oisin, inspite of his old age and lack of strength takes leave of St. Patrick and says:

> Put the staff in my hands; for I go to the
> Fenians, O cleric to chaunt
>
> The war-songs that roused them of old; they
> will rise making clouds with their breath,
>
> Innumerable, singing, exultant; the clay
> underneath them shall pant,
>
> And demons be broken in pieces, and trampled beneath
> them in death. (*C.P.* 445)

The word "Fenians" is ambiguous; it refers to both the Fenians of the ancient times and the Fenians of Yeats's time. The intention of the poet is obvious: he wants the Fenians to drive out the foreign rulers from his land through armed struggle:

> We will tear out the flaming stones, and batter
> the gateway of brass
> And enter, and sayeth 'No' when there enters
> the strongly armed guest;
> Make clean as a broom cleans, and march
> on as oxen move over young grass;
> Then feast, making converse of wars,
> and of old wounds, and turn to our rest.
>
> (*C.P.* 446)

II

The next volume *The Rose,* published in 1893, advances towards a clearer expression of Yeats's nationalism and involvement in politics. Those readers who interpret his poetry with the help of "pure literary" critics and are surprised to see the later Yeats so different may get their confusion cleared if they read his prose works and letters side by side. A great poet merges his personality in his poetry no doubt, but it is true that his poetry is a part of his total experience of life and we readers, must go through his speeches, conversations, and biography, besides letters and prose-writings.

The period between 1887 and 1891 was one of the decisive periods in his poetical career. He took the right decision to write poetry on Irish material and revive the ancient Ireland. He advised Elizabeth in a letter written to her on 30.1.1889:

> You will find it a good thing to make verses on Irish legends and places and so forth. It helps originality—and makes one's verses sincere, and gives one less numerous competitors—. Besides one should love best what is nearest and most interwoven with one's life.[14]

Almost the same kind of advice he gave to Katharine Tynan in a letter while describing his own activities and the plan to write a book that would introduce all the Irish writers since Thomas Moore:

> I have a good deal of work to do at present, more than I can manage, all at Irish literary subjects—which is as it should be. I wish you had made up the Irish novelists and folk-lorists. You with your ready pen would find plenty to say about them. There is a want for a short book (about 150 pages or 200) on Irish literature, lives and criticism of all the writers since Moore. It would sell largely, I hope, and do good work I am sure. Some day you or I must take it in hand. There is a great want for a just verdict on these men and their use for Ireland. I have often thought of setting about such a book and may when I have got on more with the novel writers.[15]

Although the projected book did not come out as Yeats had planned it, he was able to write a series of articles and reviews on the Irish writers in different magazines and journals. Besides, he wrote a series of articles under the head "Irish National Literature" in 1895, now happily collected in the first volume of *The Uncollected Prose of W.B. Yeats* edited by John P. Frayne. In these articles Yeats's aim was to define the tradition of Irish literature. The first article begins thus:

> Some of my countrymen include among [sic] national writers born in Ireland, but I prefer, though it greatly takes from the importance of our literature, to include only those who have written under Irish influence and of Irish subjects, when once a country has given perfect expression to itself in literature, has carried to maturity its literary tradition, its writers, no matter what they write of, carry its

influence with them, just as Carlyle remained a Scotsman when he wrote of German kings or French revolutionists, and Shakespeare an Elizabethan Englishman when he told of Coriolanus or Cressida.[16]

In his youthful exuberance Yeats was sharp and pointed. Considering Irish influence and Irish subjects as the basis of the Irish tradition he went to the extent of excluding Sterne, Swift, Burke and Berkeley from his list; it was only when he reached maturity he declared Swift, Goldsmith, Burke and Berkeley as his ancestors. One thing was important. He never liked a propagandist verse and always advocated in favour of genuine literature. In the same article he commented:

> The Irish national writers who have bulked largest in the past have been those who, because they served some political cause which could not wait, or had not enough of patience in themselves, turned away from the unfolding and developing of an Irish tradition, and borrowed the mature English methods of utterance and used them to sing of Irish wrongs or preach of Irish purposes. Their work was never quite satisfactory, for what was Irish in it looked ungainly in English garb, and what was English was never perfectly mastered, never wholly absorbed into their being.[17]

He excluded even Thomas Moore, Thomas Davis and John Mitchel, inspite of their nationalism, for the reason that they used the "English method" in their poetry and, so, failed to enrich the Irish tradition. He gave credit to Callanan for wiring a new kind of verse which might be said to be the source of the true Irish tradition. The poets who nurtured the tradition, he asserted, were Aubrey De Vere, William Allingham, Clarence Mangan and Sir Samuel Ferguson.

It is clear that Yeats in his youth favoured the "purest" Irish writers, but what is significant is that the essay gives us a good idea of the kind of poetry he was going to write. He had already writing *Wanderings of Oisin* and, now, his aim was to create a rich Irish literature having its own identity and absolutely free from the influence of the British literary tradition. Coupled with the concept of the Irish tradition was the notion of "Immortal Moods," the bearers, through literature, of a transcendental revelation."[18] He explained the term:

> Literature differs from explanatory and scientific writing in being wrought about an invisible soul;...these moods are the labourers and messengers of the Ruler of All.... Everything that can be seen, touched, measured, explained, understood, argued over is to the imaginative artist nothing more than a means, for he belongs to the invisible life, and delivers its ever new and ever ancient revelation. We hear much of his need for the restraints of reason, but the only restraint he can obey is the mysterious instinct that has made him an artist, and that teaches him to discover immortal moods in mortal desires, an undecaying hope in our trivial ambitions, a divine love in sexual passion.

This concept of mysteriousness in art and poetry stemmed from his association with theosophy and Rosiccucianism and experiments with magical symbols. He also came to believe in the existence of the Great Memory and the Great Mind of which the individual memory and the individual mind are parts. In the essay "Magic" he summarised his ideas:

> 1. That the borders of minds are ever shifting, and that many minds can flow into one another, as it were, and create or reveal a single mind, a single energy.
>
> 2. That the borders of our memories are as shifting, and that our memories are a part of one great memory, the memory of Nature herself.
>
> 3. That this great mind and great memory could be evoked by symbols.[19]

Yeats's concept of the great mind and the great memory compares favourably with Jung's concept of the collective unconscious and its contents, the archetypes or primordial images. Jung, too, was interested in the visions of creative writers, neurotics, *yogis* and saints and like Yeats interpreted the symbols of a vision or a dream as a part or sometimes the whole of the archetype.*

---

* For details, *see* C.G. Jung, "Archetypes of the Collective Unconscious," *Twentieth Century Criticism: The Major Statements,* William J. Handy, and Max Westbrook, ed., (Delhi: Life & Light Publishers, 1976) 205-32.

Yeats thought if there could be the great mind and the great memory, every nation must possess a mind and a memory of its own, independent of individual minds and memories. This idea led him to develop the concept of the "Unity of Culture" and the "Unity of Being." By the Unity of Being Yeats means "an image or bundle of related images symbolical or evocative of the state of mind" which unifies nations, races and individuals together. He further explains the term in *Autobiographies*:

> I thought that in man and race alike there is something called 'Unity of Being' using that term as Dante used it when he compared beauty in the *convito* to a perfectly proportioned human body.[20]

The "Unity of Being" was achieved, he continues, in the time of Homer first and then of Dante when Europe was integrated and nations, races and individuals were unified by a single image. But the process of disintegration started from Shakespeare's time and reached its finality in the twentieth century. To gain the Unity of Being again there was the need of the reversal of the process of disintegration which could be done by means of a new kind of literature. The new literature would have its base in mythology and folk-tales—"I thought that all art should be a Centaur finding in the popular lore its back and its strong legs."[21] Literature for the young nationalist was a noble means for the revival of Ireland, a socio-political aim, but never cheap or blatantly propagandist; it had to be revelatory:

> Have not all races had their first unity from a mythology that marries them to rock and hill? We had in Ireland imaginative stories, which the educated classes, rediscovering for the work's sake what I have called 'the applied arts of literature,' the association of literature, that is, with music, speech and dance; and at last, it might be, *so deepen the political passion of the nation** that, artist and poet, craftsman and daylabourer would accept a common design.[22]

The poems in *The Rose* are certainly symbolical and a large number of scholars and critics have laboured hard to trace their

---

* Italics mine.

sources for an adequate interpretation but have forgotten to add the fact that the symbols, having their source in the Irish mythology and folk-tales, are used to evoke the image that unifies the nation, the race and the individuals, certainly a political aim. In the poem "The Rose upon the Rood Of Time" Yeats invokes the symbolical rose:

> Red Rose, Proud Rose, sad Rose of all my days!
> Come near me, while I sing the ancient ways. (*C.P.* 35)

After the invocation, he narrates the deeds of the legendary Irish heroes. He wishes the rose to come nearer to him so that he will not be misled by petty things; but not so near to make him almost breathless by its powerful influence:

> Come near, come near, come near—Ah leave me still
> A little pace for the rose-breath to fill:
> Lest I may no more hear common things that crave.
> (*C.P.* 35)

The poems "Fergus and the Druid" and "Cuchulain's Fight With The Sea" are ancient legends transmuted into fine poetry. Following the footprints of Mangan and Ferguson, Yeats demonstrates the difference between the decadent English poetry of the eighteen nineties and the energetic Irish poetry of that period. John Unterecker rightly comments:

> 'Fergus and the Druid' and 'Cuchulain's Fight With The Sea' are with *Oisin,* Yeats's first important poetic contributions to that Unity of Culture which he hoped to impose on Ireland by making her familiar with her own legends.[23]

"The Lake Isle of Innisfree" one of the most anthologised poems of Yeats is essentially a longing for Sligo, although it has been interpreted, and rightly so, as man's desire for peace and happiness in this world of hurry and scurry. Earlier it was believed that Innisfree was an imaginary island. Now we all know that it is not so, Yeats tells how he came to write this poem:

> I had still the ambition, formed in Sligo in my teens of living in imitation of Thoreau on Innisfree, a little island in Lough Gill, and when walking through Fleet Street very

> homesick I heard a little tinkle of water and saw a fountain in a shop-window which balanced a little ball upon its jet, and began to remember lake waters. From the sudden remembrance came my poem 'Innisfree' my first lyric with anything in its rhythm of my own music.[24]

This remembrance was actually the revival of his past experience. When he was a child he had seen Innisfree and heard a popular story about it. Once he went alone to sleep in a wood near the island. He has described the reason why he wanted to go to Innisfree and build a cottage there:

> My father had read to me some passage out of *Walden*, and I planned to live some day in a cottage on a little island called Innisfree, and Innisfree was opposite Slish Wood where I meant to sleep.[25]

Apart from its music and lyricism, the poem is an important achievement of the young poet. Although he says in *Autobiographies* that it was written because he felt sick, there is no trace of morbidity; on the other hand it is a poem of joy that inspires us all to spend some time in the lap of nature to ease the tension of our busy life.

Till 1891 Yeats was full of high hopes and was sure that under the leadership of Charles Parnell Ireland would gain freedom and he, W.B. Yeats, would be able to make his country achieve "unity of culture" by means of literature. The poems which he wrote during this period are highly optimistic and sing the glory of ancient Ireland. He deliberately linked Sligo and the places around it with the legendary and mythical figures to arouse patriotic feelings. He was successful in his attempt to a large extent. It is true that his dream of reviving the "unity of culture" remained unrealised but he did free Irish literature from the influence of the English tradition and brought it to the level of other European literatures.

The poems of this period, because of their enthusiasm and romanticism, are the product of the Celtic Twilight. The poem "Into the Twilight" best represents the hopeful, enthusiastic, zealous young Yeats who had begun his poetical career with the lofty ideal of Irish nationalism:

Out-worn heart in a time out-worn,
Come clear of the nets of wrong and right;
Laugh, heart, again in the grey twilight,
Sigh, heart, again in the dew of morn.

Young mother Eire is always young
Dew ever shining and twilight grey. (*C.P.* 65)

The optimism of the Celtic Twilight did not last long. The stern realities of the period after Parnell's fall changed his outlook. Current Irish politics made him a man of experience.

REFERENCES

1. John P. Frayne, ed., *Uncollected Prose* By W.B. Yeats, Vol. I. 147.
2. *Ibid.*, 162.
3. *Ibid.*, 177.
4. *Autobiographies*, 82.
5. John Unterecker, *A Reader's Guide to W.B. Yeats*, (London: Thames and Hudson, 1959), 73.
6. David Daiches, "The Earlier Poems: Some Themes and Patterns," *In Excited Reverie*, ed., A.N. Jeffares and K.G.W. Cross, (London: Macmillan, 1965), 49.
7. A.N. Jeffares, *A Commentary on the Collected Poems of W.B. Yeats*, (London: Macmillan, 1968), 13.
8. *Ibid.*, 13.
9. *Ibid.*, 14.
10. A. Wade ed., *The Letters of W.B. Yeats*, 33.
11. *Collected Poems*, "Notes," 538.
12. R. Fallis, *The Irish Renaissance*, 53.
13. R. Ellmann, *Yeats: The Man and The Masks*, 53.
14. A Wade, ed., *The Letters of W.B. Yeats*, 104.
15. *Ibid.*, 133.
16. John P. Frayne, *Uncollected Prose By W.B. Yeats.*, Vol. I, 360.
17. *Ibid.*, 361.
18. *Ibid.*, 367.
19. *Essays and Inroductions*, 28.
20. *Autobiographies*, 190.
21. *Ibid.*, 191.
22. *Ibid.*, 194.
23. John Unterecker, *A Reader's Guide to W.B. Yeats*, 78.
24. *Autobiographies*, 153.
25. *Ibid.*, 71-72.

3

AFTER PARNELL

I

Till 1890 Yeats was romantically optimistic. He writes in *Autobiographies* that he had high hopes of uniting Ireland culturally and his hopes were further raised when his country began to revive its glory and could stand on its own under the able leadership of Charles Parnell:

> I had seen Ireland in my own time turn from the bragging rhetoric and gregarious humour of O'Connell's generation and school, and after herself to the solitary and proud Parnell as to her anti-self, buskin followed hand on sock, and I had begun to hope, or to half-hope, that we might be the first in Europe to seek unity as deliberately as it had been sought by theologian, poet, sculptor, architect from the eleventh to the thirteenth century.[1]

But Parnell's tragic death on 6 October 1891 shocked him. The death was a blow to him but what was more disturbing was the betrayal of the Irish people in Parnell's dire need. Captain O'Shea filed a case against Charles Parnell for his involvement with Mrs. O'Shea without obtaining a divorce. The case caused a great furore and gave an opportunity to the British government to depose him from his leadership in the Irish Parliament. The Irish Parliamentary party stood by him and supported him as Chairman at first but later on yielded to the pressure of the British Prime-Minister W.E. Gladstone. After the party's withdrawal of support, Gladstone took no time in deposing Parnell of Chairmanship. The inscrutable and proud Parnell could not bear the betrayal; he broke down and died six months thereafter. This betrayal angered Yeats. He said that it was an act of cowardice on the part of the Irish people to withdraw their support when Parnell was fighting superbly for Ireland's liberation. The ground for his deposition was equally flimsy and smacked of fundamentalism:

> The Bishops and the Party
> That tragic story made,
> A husband that had sold his wife
> And after that betrayed. (*C.P.* 356)

He felt that the nation's unity was broken and that his plan to revive the unity of culture was nipped in the bud.

Parnell's death marked the end of an era noted for its heroic leaders, at least in Yeats's eyes, and the events that followed it culminated in the division of leaders into two factions, the Parnellites and the anti-Parnellites, the latter commanding the majority. The Irish intellectuals reacted sharply against mean politics and began to revive literary activities for uniting the nation. Yeats, shocked and embittered, engaged himself in literary activities solely to raise Ireland's image. Three days before Parnell's death, he had briefly explained his project in the article "The Young Ireland League" published in the magazine *United Ireland,* 3 October 1891:

> We are Fenians coming to take care of Mr. Parnell.... It really seems needful to say that our aim is to help or train up a nation of worthy men and women who shall be able to work for public good, whether we are about to win an Irish Parliament or whether the old war against English dominion is still to go on. The general election,* or the coming of Home Rule itself, will not do away with the need for our work, for our enemies are ignorance and bigotry and fanaticism, the eternal foes of the human race which may not be abolished in any way by the Acts of Parliament.[2]

Perhaps, it will not be a eulogy if we admire Yeats's vision. India, after fifty-five years of independence, is still torn by the

---

* John P. Frayne comments: "In the general election of July 1892, Gladstone's Liberal Party won a majority. In 1893, a Home Rule Bill was passed by the House of Commons, but it was rejected by the House of Lords, *Uncollected Prose.*

fanaticism of different groups and the right-thinking people are disturbed by the evil effects of communalism and terrorism; the whole country is divided on the basis of caste, region and religion. Yeats was quite right when he said that the Irish people had to be properly educated through the best literature of Ireland to learn the lesson of national integration and combat ignorance and fanaticism.

David Daiches rightly called him a 'practical visionary'*. The following passage from the same article of Yeats gives the idea how practical he was in the implementation of his programme.

> To do this work of ours we seek to revive certain educational instruments—the Young Ireland Societies—that proved effective in the past and at the same time to do away with various defects which we have learned to remedy by experience.[3]
>
> * * *
>
> The actual work before the League is definite enough. Classes will be organized to teach the history and language of Ireland, lectures will be given upon Irish subjects, and most important of all, reading-rooms will be started in connection with the various branches. They need not cost much. It has been calculated that a reading-room, where the papers of all sides and the best magazines are taken can be kept going on in a country village for 4s or 5s.[4]

Being a practical visionary, Yeats began the project he had outlined in the article "The Young Ireland." He founded the Irish Literary Society in London and Dublin first. The old Southwark Irish Literary Society that had been established for the spread of Irish literature did little for achieving the desired goal because the workers were lazy and half-serious. Luckily, its members invited Yeats to speak on Irish literature. Yeats's lecture impressed the listeners as it was free from quotations and narrative digressions. This success accentuated his activities.

John O'Leary and Maud Gonne actively supported him in launching and functioning of the new literary programme. Their

* David Daiches, "The Practical Visionary," *Encounter*, Vol. XIX, No. 3 (Sept. 1962).

support was timely and important in view of the criticism which some of the London and Dublin people made against him. The Dublin people considered his view of life too remote from the national struggle and, in London, the Rhymers felt that he was wasting his gifts and time on the Irish literary politics. He criticised the Rhymers' view of poetry for poetry's sake. He took the right path by rejecting the Rhymers' sole concern with "the cadence of music and beauty of phrase" and the propagandist verse of the lesser Irish poets. He wrote in the essay "Hopes and Fears for Irish Literature":

> When I talk to the people of literary ambition here in Ireland, I find them holding that literature must be the expression of conviction and be the garment of noble emotion and not an end in itself.... But side by side with this robustness and rough energy of ours there goes most utter indifference to art, the most dire careless, the most inter-mixture of the commonplace.[5]

Yeats's aim was to develop Irish literature not the way the sentimental Irish poets wanted nor the way the Rhymers practised; he wanted Irish literature to be autonomous, not a part of politics, and deeply rooted in life. He advised his people to distinguish themselves from the younger generation of poets in France and England and exhorted them to study the history of Ireland and write poetry and drama taking inspiration from old legends and popular folk-tales:

> We have behind us in the past the most moving legends and a history of lofty passions. If we can but take that history and those legends and turn them into dramas, poems, and stories full of the living soul of the present, and make them massive with conviction and profound with reverie, we may deliver that new great utterance for which the world is waiting.[6]

After defining his idea of Irish literature, he launched the programme vigorously. He was able to draw the attention of the great literary men of his time to the newly founded the National Literary Society in London. Soon John O'Leary, J.P. Taylor, Douglas Hyde, Dr. Sigerson, Count Plunkett, Dr. Coffey, George Coffey, Patrick J. McCall and Richard Ashe King joined it. Almost all the Irish literary men were in favour of creating an independent Irish literature which, though written in English, would be free from the influence of the English tradition. Dr. Douglas Hyde in his speech "The De-Anglicising of Ireland" delivered on December 2, 1892 appealed to the Irish people to substitute Gaelic for all English things. Showing his agreement Yeats wrote in his letter to the editor of the *United Ireland.*

> I agree with every word you said last week about Dr. Hyde's lecture, and, like many others, am deeply grateful to you for your reprint of it in the current number...it seems to me the best possible augury for the success of the movement we are trying to create.[7]

Although Yeats was a nationalist to the core, he was not to be guided by parochialism. He did not agree with Dr. Hyde on his insistence on the full adoption of Gaelic and complete exclusion of English. He boldly affirmed that it was more practical to use English language at the place of Gaelic which was limited to a few people and argued that what was important was the content, not language. He pleaded that the Irish spirit could be effectively asserted in English which was being largely and creatively used in Ireland. Naming a few important books written in English he made a fervent appeal to the Irish people:

> Let us make these books and the books of our older writers known among the people and we will do more to de-Anglicise Ireland than by longing to recall the Gaelic tongue and the snows of yesteryear. Let us by all means prevent the decay of that tongue where we can, and preserve it always among us as a learned language to be a fountain of nationality in our midst, but do not let us base upon it our hope of nationhood.[8]

Through the National Literary Society Yeats wanted to create a national literature which could compare favourably with the great literatures of the world. The dispute between the National Literary Society members and the Young Irelanders arose for the reason that the latter favoured publication of patriotic verses to arouse the revolutionary ideas whereas Yeats was against propagandist verse. The result of the dispute was harmful to both sides but more to Yeats. He was thoroughly misunderstood and it took a long time for him to rehabilitate himself as a nationalist and true son of the soil. Nevertheless, he defended his position stoutly during the period of controversy and outlined in clear terms his idea of the Irish national literature in his lecture on 19 May, 1893 which was later printed in the *United Ireland,* 27 May, 1893. John P. Frayne has summarised and evaluated the lecture sympathetically. I quote the first two paragraphs of his evaluation:

> It is the most candid and developed expression of Yeats's hopes for Irish literature in the early nineties.
>
> One may read this lecture as an answer to the two groups of adversaries: the first represented by John F. Taylor, believed that oratory and rhetorical and polemical poetry were the supreme Irish literary arts. Yeats disliked oratory and he believed that such indulgence in rhetoric had destroyed the Young Ireland movement of 1848. The second group were those Irish literary patriots who believed that Irish writing should be judged by Ireland alone and hence English or continental criticism was irrelevant. Yeats also thought that Irish writing should be the product of as intense a national or local feeling as possible but that only a study of great works of literature by foreigners such as Homer and Balzac could save the Irish writers of his own time from becoming locally reversed mediocrities. Although he wanted young Irish writers to study other literatures, he tried to separate Irish from English literature, especially since he implied that English literature was in death throes—an assertion which would make true Irish patriots forgive Yeats for censuring native literary slovenliness.[9]

After defining the concept of Irish literature Yeats accelerated the pace of his literary activities. But there was another trouble ready to disturb his plans. Gavan Duffy, a comrade of Davis, returned from Australia after a long exile. He soon planned to publish a series of books of the still unpublished writers of the Young Ireland Society. The plan alarmed Yeats because, he feared, his project of publishing books written by young writers would fail if Duffy were allowed to go on with his plan. Yeats opposed Duffy. Duffy and Rolleston tried to persuade T. Fisher Unwin and his reader, Edward Garnett, to publish their series of

Irish writers. Edward Garnett, a well-meaning man and lover of the Irish cause, did his best to soothe both the parties. He wrote a long letter to Yeats, explaining that there was not much difference between him and Rolleston:

> The fact is the whole issue of the split lies between you and Rolleston. If you and he would join hands (you representing the Parnellite party, and Rolleston the London Irish Literary Society) you would find that you and he are practically of the same mind about the books and that *your own ideas would* be carried through.

In the postcript of the same letter he added,

> Let Duffy be the English Monarch, and you and Rolleston the joint Prime Ministers.
>
> It's always on one or two men who *work* for a thing that the issue depends. Now Rolleston and you are the prime movers, and the question depends on *your* good feeling.[10]

Thus Edward Garnett solved the problem and it was decided that T. Fisher Unwin would publish books of both the parties in the same series.

Yeats's idea of Irish literature that it should have its base in the native soil but absorb the best of European literature made the young writers think in a new way and give up parochialism. Now in retrospect, we cannot but admire Yeats's maturity even at the young age of thirty-seven. But this maturity came to him after his active participation in politics. Recollecting his activities in National Literary Society he wrote:

> The great numbers of those who joined my society had come earlier under the seal of Young Ireland at that age when we were all mere wax; the more ambitious had gone daily to some public library to read the bound volumes of Thomas Davis's old newspaper, and tried to see the world as Davis saw it. No philosophic speculation, *no economic question of the day** disturbed an orthodoxy which unlike that of religion, had no philosophic history and the religious bigot was glad that it should be so.[11]

This passage makes it amply clear that Yeats wanted economic and philosophic questions to be discussed in literature

* Italics mine.

because without these, he sincerely felt, no creative writer was able to understand man in society and his place in the universe. Thomas Davis could write sentimental poetry with patriotic fervour but what he needed was a philosophy to give his poetry enduring quality.

Yeats published *The Fairy and Folk Tales of the Irish Peasantry* and a two volume anthology *Selection from the Irish Novelists* in 1893. The poem "The Dedication to a Book of Stories" is in praise of the novelists included in the *Selection.* It begins with a sad remembrance of Ireland's glorious past when literature, symbolised here by the "green branch with many a bell," flourished luxuriantly:

> There was a green branch hung with many a bell
> When her own people ruled their tragic Eire;
>
> And from its murmuring greenness, calm of Faery,
> A Druid calmness, on all hearers fell.

(*C.P.* 51)

In the next stanza he describes the effect of the Druid* calmness that poetry exercised on the Irish people:

> It charmed away the merchant from his guile,
> And turned the farmer's memory from his cattle,
> And humbled in sleep the roaring ranks of battle
> And all grew friendly a little while. (*C.P.* 51)

He is sad that at present the neglect of the "green branch," the uniting image, has led to the disintegration of Ireland. He, therefore, resolves to revive the glory of Ireland, symbolised by the "tree." He invokes the bells, symbols of creative writers, to ring merrily to revive the old glory:

> ...gay bells bring laughter
> That shakes a mouldering cobweb from the rafter
> And yet the saddest chimes are best enjoyed.

(*C.P.* 51)

"To Ireland in the Coming Times" is a defence of his position as a poet. Jeffares and Stock have argued that the poem is a reply to the charge levelled against him by Maud Gonne that he was

---

* The Druids were an order of priests among the ancient Celts of Gaul and Britain.

indifferent to Ireland's cause. The poem begins with the positive assertion that he is equally active for Ireland's cause and ready to act for her liberation as the other members of the Young Ireland Society and Fenian Brotherhood are:

> Know that I would accounted be
> True brother of a company
> That sang, to sweeten Ireland's wrong
> Ballad and story, rann and song; (*C.P.* 56)

He explains his position unequivocally that he is following the line of Thomas Davis, Clarence Mangan and Samuel Ferguson, the great patriots who were deeply concerned with both political and cultural independence of Ireland:

> Nor may I less be counted one
> With Davis, Mangan, Ferguson
> Because to him who ponders well,
> My rhymes more than their rhyming tell
> Of things discovered in the deep,
> Where only body's laid asleep. (*C.P.* 57)

"To Ireland in the Coming Times" is more than an apology:

> I cast my heart into my rhyme
> That you, in the dim coming times,
> May know how my heart went with them
> After the red-rose-bordered hem. (*C.P.* 58)

John P. Frayne while analysing Yeats's nationalism in the essay "The Twilight Propaganda" makes the following comment on his efforts for the Celtic revival. The comment fully explains the theme and purpose of "To Ireland in the Coming Times":

> In Yeats's first poetic testament, "To Ireland in the Coming Times" (1892), he claimed his place in the company of poets who sang "to sweeten Ireland's wrong." The wrong which England had done to Ireland was, in Yeats's opinion, cultural and literary as well as political and economic. From the outset of his career, Yeats tried to avenge the neglect of Anglo-Irish literature shown by English critics and Irish intellectuals* alike. To achieve this task, Yeats attempted to mould the broken and shattered fragments of a half-

* *See* Yeats's essay "Professor Dowden and Irish Literature," *Uncollected Prose*, Vol. I, 346-54.

> forgotten tradition and thereby make the world believe that Ireland possessed an important literature.[12]

Although Yeats's conception of literature was valid by the standards of his time, he could not write the kind of poetry which we call modern. The first reason for writing unsubstantial and dreamy poetry is that Yeats did not have a great Irish poet behind him to guide and he had to grope in darkness to find the true path. He confessed his weakness later:

> Metrical composition is always very difficult for me, nothing is done upon the first day, not one rhyme is in its place, and when at last the rhymes begin to come, the first rough draft of a six-line stanza takes the whole day. At that time I had not formed a style, and sometimes a six-line stanza would take several days, and not seem finished then;....[13]

The second reason and this is equally important is that he then believed in the mysteriousness of art and poetry and ignored the importance of the stark realities of day-to-day life, the realities which harden our spirit and give substance to our language. In his youth Yeats believed:

> Everything that can be seen, touched, measured, explained, understood, argued over, is to the imaginative artist nothing more than a means, for he belongs to the invisible life, and delivers its ever new and its ever ancient revelation.[14]

In another essay he expressed his love for thinness and faint impressions:

> I see, indeed, in the arts of every country those faint lights and faint colours and faint outlines and faint energies which many call 'the decadence' and which I, because I believe that arts lie dreaming of things to come, prefer to call the autumn of the body.[15]

It is this fascination of faint colours, faint dreams and faint energy that dilutes the vitality of his early poetry. "The Hosting of the Sidhe," the first poem in the volume *The Wind Among the Reeds* (1893), is written under the influence of the Rhymers. Although Yeats sings of the people of ancient myths and folk-tales, he fails to relate the past with the present and is lost in a dreamland of heart's desire:

And Niamh calling Away, come away;
Empty your heart of its mortal dream.
The winds awaken, the leaves whirl round,
Our cheeks are pale, our hair is unbound,
Our breasts are heaving, our eyes are agleam
Our arms waving, our lips are apart. (*C.P.* 61)

Here the phrases "mortal dream," "pale cheeks," "heaving breasts," "eyes agleam," "arms waving," "lips apart" and "hair unbound" make the poem escapist in tone. If we accept Freud's interpretation, these are the images of a neurotic's fantasy. It seems that the pale young sick lover expresses his longing for women who are unapproachable being part of a dream.

The dream of love for another world is evident in "The Hosting of the Air," where the lover, like the knight of "La Belle Dame Sans Merci" falls in love with a fairy only to be deceived in the end:

O' Driscoll scattered the cards
And out of his dream awoke.
Old men and young men and young girls
Were gone like drifting smoke. (*C.P.* 64)

It is generally said[16] that it was Maud Gonne's rejection of his proposal for marriage that contributed to the gloom of the love poems Yeats write in the eighteen-nineties but we have also to take note of the fact that the poems written on Maud Gonne and the unrequited love in the later period are free from the kind of gloom and melancholy of the early period. In fact, frustration in love had little to do with the quality of his poetry as he had already formulated the theory that poetry should be about faint colours, faint energy and faint desires. He could write sinewy prose in that period because politics demands energy but when writing of poetry came he followed his friends Lionel Johnson and Ernest Dowson. The poems in the volume *The Wind Among the Reeds* can be remembered for the culmination of the early style Yeats practised at the Rhymers' club. They bear testimony to his declaration in the following quatrain:

God loves dim ways of glint and gleam
To please him well my rhyme must be

> A dyed and figured mystery.
> Thought hid in thought, dream hid in dream.[17]

New experience, mainly political, made Yeats revise his idea of poetry and write in a new way. He found that Allingham and Ferguson could not help him much nor the Victorians. While he was at cross-roads, Arthur Symons introduced him to the French symbolist movement in literature. Although he knew French very little he read Mallarmé, Verlaine and Count Villiers de L'Isle Adam with great interest and learnt from them how to use symbols systematically in poetry:

> He [Arthur Symons] was making those translations from Mallarmé and Verlaine, from Calderon, from Saint John of the Cross, which are the most accomplished metrical translations of our time, and I think that those from Mallarmé may have given elaborate form to my verses of those years to the latter poems of *The Wind Among the Reeds* to *The Shadowy Waters,* while Villiers de L'Isle Adam had shaped whatever in my *Rosa Alchemica* Pater had not shaped.[18]

However, Yeats never became a disciple of Mallarmé as some critics have claimed nor did he follow exactly the French tradition. Rooted in his native soil and eager to distinguish Irish Literary tradition from the English or the French, he took symbols from the Irish mythology and avoided the use of private symbols as practised by the French symbolists and later on, as Bowra has pointed out, made symbols of real persons in the Irish history. Besides, he found in his occultist experiments that symbols had effects independent of their sources or the intention of the conscious. This discovery led him to the idea that behind every symbol were the forces of the elemental powers and that symbols evoked indefinable feelings in the reader:

> All art that is not mere story-telling or mere portraiture, is symbolic, and has the purpose of those symbolic talismans which mediaeval magicians made with complex colours and forms, and bade their patients ponder daily, and guard with holy secrecy; for it entangles in complex colours and forms, a part of the Divine Essence.[19]

* * *

> All sounds, all colours, all forms, either because of long associations evoke indefinable and yet precise emotions, or, as I prefer to think, call down upon us certain disembodied powers whose footsteps over our hearts we call emotions; and when sound, and colour, and form are in a musical relation, a beautiful relation to one another, they become as it were, one sound, one colour, one form, and evoke an emotion that is made out of their distinct evocations and yet is one emotion.[20]

Yeats divides symbols into two groups, though the division is arbitrary and groups overlap each other. In the first group are the emotional symbols which evoke emotions only and in the second group are the intellectual symbols which evoke ideas alone or ideas mixed with emotions.[21] For a full appreciation of a poem, there is the need of intellect without which no reader can pass through the state of trance, the state of poetic creation. He writes:

> It is the intellect that decides where the reader shall ponder over the procession of symbols, and if the symbols are merely emotional, he gazes from amid the accidents and destinies of the world; but if the symbols are intellectual too, he becomes himself a part of pure intellect, and he is himself mingled with the procession.[22]

We may conclude with Yeats that only symbolic poetry is capable of evoking the desired emotions in the reader and can enable him or her to achieve the unity of being, the image which unifies nations, races and individuals together.

Uptill *The Wind Among the Reeds* Yeats's poetic diction, inspite of his intention was vague; the French symbolists provided him the means to express his complex, feelings and emotions concretely. Intellect, neglected uptill now, begins to play an important role in poetic creation.

In the "Song of Wandering Aengus" the legendary character is not a shadowy individual but a symbol which concretises the pangs of a dejected lover who wishes to:

...pluck till time and times are done
The silver apples of the moon
The golden apples of the sun. (*C.P.* 67)

The white deer of "He Mourns for the Change" is explicitly used as the symbol of the lady-love, the "hound with one red ear" the lover and the "Boar without Bristles" of death:

I would that the Boar without bristles had come
from the West
And had routed the sun and moon and the stars
out of the sky
And lay in the darkness, grunting, and turning to rest.
(*C.P.* 68)

However, the best in the volume are the political poems where symbols are used with great precision and which evoke multiplicity of emotions. "The Valley of the Black Pig" is a prophetic poem in which the destruction of Ireland's enemies is envisioned. "All Over Ireland," writes Yeats in the "Notes," "there are prophesies of the complete rout of the enemies of Ireland, in a certain valley of the Black Pig and these prophesies are, no doubt, now, as they were in the Fenian days, a political force. I have heard of one man who would not give any money to the Land League, because the battle could not be until the close of the century; but as a rule, periods of trouble bring prophecies of its near coming."[23]

The "Black Pig" symbolises the elemental powers that will destroy Ireland's enemies. The poem is a vision of a fierce fight between two armies, obviously of Ireland and England. The defeat of the enemy side raises the hope that a day will come when Ireland is free and independent of the foreign rule.

The best poem is "The Secret Rose" which was first published as an introduction to the stories *The Secret Rose* (1897). The "rose" here is something too vast and exalted to be expressed in words, and is much richer in meaning than that given by Yeats in the "Notes;" it is sometimes eternal beauty, sometimes intellectual beauty and sometimes the blessed moment. According to Jeffares, and his interpretation is certainly the best, this poem perfectly combines Yeats's all the three aspirations: gain of Maud Gonne's love, success in magic and writing of poetry with its background in the Irish history. He writes:

> This spiritual beauty was soon as part of Yeats's own belief that there would be revelation, due to the creation of Celtic mysteries (and a complete understanding between Yeats and Maud Gonne). Madam McBride has told me that Yeats, as well as symbolising spiritual beauty by the Rose, intended at times to allude to her by the symbol. Thus in "The Secret Rose" the blending of all these aspirations is built up with a wealth of imagery.[24]

Yeats invokes the "inviolate rose" to enfold him in its best hours so that he may attain the blessed moment which saints have sought in the "Holy Sepulchre" or lovers in beauty. The next aspiration is for the moment when the "invisible" gates would open for him as they opened for Blake, Boehme and Swedenborg,[25] and when his "philosophy would find its manuals of devotion in all imaginative literature, and set before Irishmen for special manual on Irish literature which, though made by many minds would seem the work of a single mind, and turn our places of beauty or legendary association into holy symbols."[26]

After the invocation, he proceeds to present a panorama of the Irish history:

> And the king whose eyes
> Saw the Pierced Hands and Roods of elder rise
> In Druid vapour and make the torches dim;
> Till vain frenzy awoke and he died; and him
> Who met Fand walking among flaming dew
> By a grey shore where the wind never blew,
> And lost the world and Emer for a kiss. (*C.P.* 77)

At the end, he, like William Blake, waits eagerly for the fulfilment of his aspirations:

> I, too, await
> The hour of thy great wind of love and hate
> When shall the stars be blown about the sky,
> Like the sparks blown out of a smithy and die?
> Surely thine hour has come, thy great wind blows,
> Far off, most secret, and inviolate Rose? (*C.P.* 78)

The poems in *The Wind Among the Reeds* lack what we call solidity and strength. C.M. Bowra rightly comments:

> In *The Wind Among the Reeds* Yeats adapted the symbolist method to his own views and uses. It suited his own temperament, his deep trust in dreams and visions. It suited his belief that a poet is a kind of medium between spirit and men, a seer who interprets clues to the mystery of life. Yet, his masculine intelligence demanded a more concrete and vigorous style with a greater precision and force.[27]

Surely Yeats was not satisfied with his performance in *The Wind Among the Reeds,* inspite of the successful use of symbols. The reason, he rightly felt, was that he had failed to develop a terse and forceful style that could carry the load of his complex thoughts and experiences.

II

After Parnell's death, Yeats did not give up politics entirely. He cherished the hope of reviving the heroic Ireland. He continued to support the Parnellite group in politics. However, he focused his attention more to literature for, he felt, cultural revival was as important as political independence. Yeats's biographers[28] have laid too much emphasis on his involvement with Maud Gonne and maintained that Yeats's participation in Irish politics was just a covert means to win her love. Nothing can be farther from the truth.* By 1897 Yeats had become a famous poet and he knew what was right and what was wrong for him. A sincere nationalist like him would not change his views for the sake of love. In fact he was a nationalist before meeting Maud in John O'Leary's house. It was John O'Leary who initiated him in active politics. During the period of his friendship with her he never subscribed wholly to her views. Maud Gonne always favoured underground activities of violence and bloodshed but Yeats opposed this point of view and said

* Professor Ellmann has refuted this view of biographers. He comments: "In his plans, he later confessed self-deprecatingly, 'there was much patriotism and more desire for a fair woman [...].' But we should not allow his own confession of a multiplicity of motives to blind us to the larger idealism which animated all that he did for his country." *Yeats: The Man and the Masks,* 106.

that unnecessary violence and bloodshed would not help Ireland win freedom.

After becoming a member of the Irish Republican Brotherhood, a secret organization descending from the Fenian movement, he planned to establish a theatre that would produce good plays based on Irish legends and myths for accentuating nationalist feeling and reviving Ireland's cultural identity. The situation was very encouraging. The American revolutionaries* had split into two factions: the Triangle and the Devoy. The Devoy accussed the Triangle of murdering Cronin, one of their leaders. Yeats describes the effect of the murder in Ireland:

> A prominent American had been murdered for political reasons and another Irish-American had been tried and acquitted, but was still accused by his political opponents and the dispute had spread to London and to Ireland, and had there intermixed itself with current politics and gathered new bitterness. My committee and the majority of the Nationalist Irish societies throughout England were upon one side, and the Dublin Committee and the majority of the Nationalist societies in Ireland upon the other, and feeling ran high.[29]

The young Dublin Nationalists planned a monument to Wolfe Tone. They formed the Commemoration Committee but did not find an acceptable President. Yeats thought if he accepted the chairmanship of the Association he might be able to prevent a public quarrel and, so, "make a great central council possible."[30] He hoped for a grand plan. In the words of A.N. Jeffares:

> It seemed possible to Yeats that after laying of the stone all the Irish parties could be invited to subordinate themselves to his Council of English Wolfe Tone Association which would then be, after careful re-election on a more permanent basis, the equivalent of an Irish Parliament for it would control the coming and going of the Irish members at the Westminster and would have great strength.

Ably supported by Maud Gonne, Yeats went to different places to deliver lectures for collection of funds. He talked to Michael

* The Irish revolutionaries who had emigrated to America.

Davitt, leader of the Land League, on the current political issues, especially the quarrel between the Parnellites and the anti-Parnellites but found that he paid little attention to the points raised by him. He felt that Davitt was a man of contemplation, not of action and his Land League was a movement to satisfy his personal aspirations and had little to do with the nation's welfare. He seriously began to think of a national movement in which all the different factions would merge and this could be done by inviting the Parnellite and the anti-Parnellite groups to attend the foundation-stone laying or Wolfe Tone's statue's unveiling ceremony. He also decided to invite the Unionists who had started agitation against over-taxation. He hoped if such a unity between different political groups was made, some wild Fenian movement might begin. But his plan was ruined by the treachery of Frank Hugh O'Donnell. A.N. Jeffares gives a detailed account of the episode:

> Yeats had been granted the use of a weekly column in a Dublin newspaper for the new movement and mentioned this to O'Donnell. Within a few days, before Yeats had even brought the matter before his committee, a report of the activities of some unknown secret society appeared in the column. This had nothing to do with the new movement, and when Yeats went to visit O'Donnell, who was in hospital after a gas explosion in his flat, his conversation was given the following day as a report of 'Count Shanon' an imaginary branch of the imaginary secret society.[31]

O'Donnell's venomous pamphlet damaged Yeats's plan badly and he had to abandon the project with a feeling of defeat. This failure in politics, he thought, had brought him to a critical point and he had to decide whether he should remain active in politics or go for literature alone. He decided to dissociate himself from active politics, (although he remained a Parnellite throughout his life and took part in active politics from time to time) and start the Irish Dramatic Movement. This decision was a boon to Ireland as it proved to be one of the greatest literary movements of the twentieth century; it raised Ireland to a cultural height and produced great playwrights like J.M. Synge, Lady Gregory, Sean O'Casey, Padraic Colum and provided ample opportunity to Edward Martyn and George Moore to exhibit their talents.

He founded The Irish Literary Theatre in 1897 in collaboration with Edward Martyn and Lady Gregory; a little later George Moore joined the team.* Earlier the Garlic League had planned to produce plays in the Irish language. The plan failed because it was unpractical. Yeats was right in asserting the fact that English, not Gaelic, was the language of creative writing in Ireland and it was a futile effort to write and stage plays in a language which was spoken by a few. The prospectus of the theatre made it clear that its objective was to create a new kind of audience and project a new image of Ireland. It read:

> We hope to find in Ireland an uncorrupted and imaginative audience, trained to listen by its passion for oratory—we will show that Ireland is not the home of buffoonery and of sentiments, as it has been represented but the home of an ancient idealism.[32]

Of the three, Lady Gregory was less concerned with the theory of drama. Edward Martyn, whose plays were not performed by the British theatre inspite of their intrinsic music, wanted to follow the realism of Henrik Ibsen. But Yeats was opposed to this idea; influenced by French symbolism and Indian mysticism he wanted poetic drama. The result of this dialectic of realism on one side and symbolism and mysticism on the other was the production of a new kind of drama, a drama hitherto unknown in Europe. Edward Martyn's *The Heather Field* and Yeats's *Countess Cathleen* were the first plays of this new trend which blended naturalism and symbolism. Richard Fallis comments:

> *The Heather Field* is a strong play, if sometimes stilted and derivative, in which the conflict of idealism and realism together with some effective handling of symbolism and dream make for more than an ordinary problem play.[33]

Yeats followed Martyn's idea of the theatre in *Countess Cathleen*

---

* When Lady Gregory, Mr. Edward Martyn and myself planned The Irish Literary Theatre, we decided that it should be carried on the form we had projected for three years.... A Little later George Moore joined us." W.B. Yeats, "The Irish Dramatic Movement," *Explorations*, 73.

but Martyn objected to the ending of the play. At the end of the play, Countess Cathleen, seeing her people starve to death during famine, sells her soul to Devil to save their lives. According to Martyn she should have suffered hell but, here, she goes to heaven. The final comment on her act is:

> The Light of Lights
> Looks always on the motive, not the deed,
> The Shadow of Shadows on the deed alone.[34]

For Martyn, this was too much. Before the play could be performed, he consulted an unnamed monk who denounced the play. Lady Gregory and Yeats thought that two clergymen would outvote one and, so, they consulted Father Barry and an Irish Jesuit. Father Barry supported Yeats emphatically. Martyn did not like Yeats's act and wrote him a strong latter. Now George Moore joined the fray. A radical that he was "denounced Yeats's submission of a work of art to the judgment of theologians as an act unworthy of a man of letters." Moore did not stop here. He wrote a strong letter to Edward Martyn, which offended him greatly. After a few days, Yeats met Martyn and pacified him with some judicious flattery. But the row over the play spread to many places. Now F. Hugh O'Donnell, Yeats's sworn enemy, took revenge on Yeats by publishing a pamphlet, titled *Souls for Gold* and "quoted as Yeats's own words the words of the demon merchants and represented the scene where the women barter their souls as an insult to Irish womanhood." The pamphlet provoked the press to come into action. Inspite of the attack of the press, Yeats faced the situation boldly. The play was performed on the scheduled day.

Though interpreted generally as an autobiographical play (Maud Gonne, the Countess and W.B. Yeats, Aleel), it is basically a political play with an aim to arouse nationalist feelings. The countess wins her peasants' sympathy by selling her soul for their welfare and thus establishes a new relationship between aristocracy and peasantry. The total aim of the play is to strengthen the bond of co-operation between the two and negate the existence of the middle class in Ireland; the Irish setting suggests the suffering of the Irish people during the great potato famine and the apparent help offered by the British government (the two demon merchants represent England, the "nation of shopkeepers"). The play attacks the orthodox church, too. For we, Indians, Yeats's view that it is motive which is important, is quite natural but for the church it was a heretic view in the nineteenth century. Yeats under the influence of Indian philosophy could go beyond the precincts of Christianity. Besides, he had seen how the narrow view of the church took away Parnell's life and destroyed an important cause of Ireland. The political overtone of the play is manifest.

If we leave the early controversy over *Countess Cathleen,* The Irish Literary Theatre had a promising start and soon *Maeve* by Edward Martyn, *The Last Feast of Fianna* by Alice Milligan, *Diarmuid* by George Moore and the Gaelic play *Casadh an Sugain* by Douglas Hyde were staged with great success. But soon another controversy arose. George Moore and Edward Martyn, because they were poles apart in their views, quarrelled almost everyday. When things came to a pass, they both bade farewell to the Irish Literary Theatre in 1901. After their departure, the Theatre was renamed the Irish National Theatre Society, with W.B. Yeats as President, Maud Gonne, Douglas Hyde and George Russell (A.E.) as Vice-Presidents and Frank Fay as stage Manager. Lady Gregory remained its patron.

Yeats's next important play *Cathleen-ni-Houlihan* created history. In the words of Richard Fallis:

> The Irish dramatic movement was conceived on the afternoon Yeats talked with Martyn and Lady Gregory in the great house in County Galway, but it was born at that production of *Cathleen-ni-Houlihan.*[35]

As A.N. Jeffares has pointed out, the theme of the play is taken from James Clarence Mangan's play *Kathleen-Ny-Houlihan,* a Jacobite relic translated from the Irish of William Heffernan, called William Dall or blind William.[36]

The story of the play is about Michael Gillane who forsakes his nuptial bed to join the Irish patriots who are fighting for their motherland. Michael's father is very happy because he has received a handsome dowry. While he is counting the money, he and the members of his family hear a noise outside. Unable to understand what it is all about, they look through the window and see an old women passing through the street. She looks at Michael while she passes by his house. Michael, the newly-married young man, is not willing to allow the old woman enter his house but opens the door for her on the insistence of his mother who feels pity for the old woman waiting at the door. The old woman enters the house and talks about her troubles. The family does not understand the real troubles and offers her some money, food and drink. She declines the offer and says if anybody is willing to help her, he must give her himself and all. Michael is deeply moved by her words and decides to go with her for the recovery of her green fields usurped and ravaged by foreigners. Michael's mother, Bridget, stops him from going with the old woman because he has to welcome the bride that very night. A little later, the old woman discloses her identity that she is Ireland herself, Daughter of Houlihan, and that she is not talking of ordinary things. She says:

> It is a hard service they take that help me. Many that are red-cheeked now will be pale-cheeked; many that have been free to walk the hills and bogs and the rustles will be sent to walk hard streets in far countries; many a good plan will be broken; many that have gathered money will not stay to spend it; many a child be born and there will be no father at its christening to give it a name. They that have red-cheeks will have pale-cheeks for my sake, and, for all that, they will think that they are well paid.[37]

Then she sings a song. The song has such a magic effect on Michael Gillane that he ignores his mother's advice and speaks as if he is under a spell:

> What wedding are you talking of? What clothes will I be wearing tomorrow?[38]

Then Cathleen-ni-Houlihan changes herself from an old woman to a young woman. Michael breaks away from his family and follows her to sacrifice his life for his country's sake.

The play is one of the finest expressions of Yeats's nationalism. It can be compared to Lady Gregory's *The Rising of the Moon.* In the beginning we are not aware of the intensity of the dramatic action which is going to take place at the end. There is the Gillane family almost ignorant of the troubles of

Ireland, busy in making arrangement for the welcome of the bride, Delia. It is the old woman's arrival that changes the entire scene. At the end, the play reaches the tragic sublimity. Yeats wrote to Lady Gregory after the performance:

> Last night was the most enthusiastic of all. The audience now understands *Cathleen-ni-Houlihan* and there is no difficulty in getting from humour to tragedy.[39]

Of course, the impact of the play was tremendous; it aroused intense patriotic feelings in the audience. Stephen Gwyn recollects the emotions he had while watching the drama.

> The effect of *Cathleen-ni-Houlihan* on me was that I went home asking myself if such plays should be produced unless one was prepared for people to go out to shoot and be shot.[40]

After two and half years of the premiere of *Cathleen-ni-Houlihan*, the society got a permanent theatre of its own which was named The Abbey Theatre. Expansion in activities demanded more actors and more good playwrights; J.M. Synge, Padraic Colum and William Boyle joined the company and Arthur Sinclair, George Roberts and Sara Allgood were the new actors. The fame of The Abbey Theatre spread far and wide. The great success of the Irish dramatic movement made Yeats think that his dream of uniting Ireland culturally was changing into reality; but the riots over the play *The Playboy of the Western World* made him revise his opinion. Earlier he was able to bear the mild shock he had received on the performance of *The Hour Glass* which was criticised as a heretic play. It was a mild criticism to which Yeats had answered:

> Every generation of men of letters had been called immoral by the pulpit of the newspaper, and it has been precisely when that generation has been illuminating some obscure corner of the conscience that the cry against it has been more confident.[41]

But the riot* over *The Playboy* hurt him. He criticised the prude for their narrow mindedness that prevented them from appreciating a great play. He wrote:

* The audience broke in a great fury at the word *shift* meaning chemise.

> The failure of the audience to understand this powerful and strange work (*The Playboy of the Western World*) has been the one serious failure of our movement, and it could not have happened but that the greater number of those who came to shout down the play were no regular part of our audience at all, but members of parties and societies whose main interests are political.[42]

After police intervention, the show continued peacefully. This pleased Yeats greatly and in an interview published in the *Evening Herald*, Dublin, 1 February, 1907, he said:

> Gradually the audience are beginning to see what the play means. We always had the stalls with us, but tonight for the first time we had the majority of the pit on our side, and any protests that there were perfectly fair. If members of the audience object to certain parts of the play, of course they have a perfect right to express their dissent in a reasonable way.[43]

But this satisfaction did not last long. He faced problems again in Philadelphia, U.S.A., in 1912 when the players were arrested. They were "admitted to bail and were advised by their lawyers to apply for writs of *habeas corpus* against the judge who granted warrants and to contest the constitutionality of the law under which they were arrested."[44] Later on, Yeats explained the meaning of the play in an interview and hoped that everything would be all right.[45]

How great Yeats's contribution to the Irish dramatic movement was, is aptly described by Lennox Robinson in his recollection:

> I have often had to write or speak about Lady Gregory and her work for our Theatre, and I have always said that but for her tireless interest it would have died years ago. Thinking again, I am sure, I must modify that statement... he [Yeats] always loomed in the background, an influence, a critic, and at any moment of crisis, a man of swift, forceful action. Lacking his inspiration would Lady Gregory have continued her tireless, very often unappreciated work? I doubt it.[46]

The Irish dramatic movement not only raised the intellectual and cultural level of the Irish people but also produced playwrights of the first rank like Edward Martyn, Lady Gregory, J.M. Synge, Padraic Colum, William Boyle, Lennox Robinson, Sean O'Casey, T.C. Murray and Fitzmaurice and stage artists like Fay brothers, Florence Farr, Sara Allgood, Arthur Sinclair and George Roberts. Richard Fallis evaluates the significance of the movement:

> ...the Abbey had done as much and more than any nationalist to prove that Ireland was indeed 'the home of an ancient civilization.' Yeats's plays spoke to one vision of Ireland in their intricate symbolism and passionate reverie, Lady Gregory's spoke to another, Synge's to yet a third, Colum's, Murray's, Fitzmaurice's to others still. No one vision was complete or perhaps even ultimately true, but each was a kind of truth about the Ireland that was and the Ireland that could be. Those visions, the products of the dramatic genius of Ireland's playwrights, had made drama one of the great and lasting achievements of the Irish Renaissance.[47]

If Yeats was father of the Irish dramatic movement and made the most significant contribution to Ireland's cultural identity, the movement made a significant impact on his development as a poet.

The practical realities of the theatre—management of the theatre, writing and criticising plays, politics of the audience and arrest of the actors in America—made him leave the world of the Celtic twilight and face the heat and dust of the day.* He admitted in *Autobiographies*:

> In later years, through much knowledge of the stage, through the exfoliation of my own style, I learnt that occasional prosaic words gave the impression of an active man speaking.[48]

---

* Una Ellis-Fermor comments: "In W.B. Yeats the Irish drama had not only a founder, an acute business man and a courageous fighter, but something without which these [would] have been barren, a visionary poet...." *The Irish Dramatic Movement*, (London: Methuen, 1964), 91.

* * *

> When I began to rehearse a play I had the defects of my early poetry; I insisted upon obvious all-pervading rhythm. Later on, I found myself saying that only in those lines or words where the beauty came to its climax, must rhythm be obvious.[49]

Because of the experiences both bitter and sweet and constant struggle against odds, he developed into a practical man, and courageous enough to maintain equanimity and humour even in the most trying situations. The poem "Fascination Of What Is Difficult" reveals not only Yeats's mind's workings during the controversial days but also the good humour he maintained amidst a number of setbacks:

> There's something ails our colt
> That must, as if it had not holy blood
> Nor on Olympus leaped from cloud to cloud,
> Shiver under the lash, strain, sweat and jolt
> As though it dragged road-metal. (*C.P.* 104)

What is equally important is the change in style. The frequent use of the conjunction "and" is seen no more nor the italicising of a number of lines. This poem, shortened to thirteen lines, follows the sonnet, with stanza form which slight alterations (Yeats at the time of writing it had no idea of Hopkins's curtal sonnet). It begins with the complaint that it has been a blunder on the part of the poet that he launched an ambitious project. It has:

> Dried the sap out of my veins, and rent
> Spontaneous joy and natural content
> Out of my heart. (*C.P.* 104)

Earlier the poet's imagination or creative power, like Pegasus, flew from one cloud to the other but, now, it shivers under the strain of stage management, revision of plays and rowdyism of the audience, like a horse that drags its feet while carrying heavy road-metal. He, therefore, curses his decision of doing something difficult, that is, starting the Irish dramatic movement:

> My curse on plays
> That have to be set up in fifty ways,

On the day's war with every knave and dolt,
Theatre business, management of men.
I swear before the dawn comes round again
I'll find the stable and pull out the bolt. (*C.P.* 104)

"The Fascination Of What Is Difficult" shows the direction Yeats chose for poetry. The Irish politics made him a seasoned man. "The Coming of Wisdom with Time" marks the beginning of a new era in Yeats's poetical career:

Though leaves are many, the root is one;
Through all the lying days of my youth
I swayed my leaves and flowers in the Sun
Now I may wither into the truth. (*C.P.* 105)

He did wither into the truth to germinate a new plant of poetry.

REFERENCES

1. *Autobiographies,* 195.
2. *Uncollected Prose By W. B. Yeats,* Vol. I, 206.
3. *Ibid.,* 206.
4. *Ibid.,* 207.
5. *Ibid.,* 249.
6. *Ibid.,* 250.
7. *Ibid.,* 255.
8. *Ibid.,* 256.
9. *Ibid.,* 256-67.
10. Quoted. J. Hone, *W.B. Yeats,* 98.
11. *Autobiographies,* 202.
12. John P. Frayne. "Twilight Propoganda," *Uncollected Prose,* 35.
13. A Wade, *Latters of W.B. Yeats,* 70.
14. *Essays and Introductions,* 195.
15. *Ibid.,* 191.
16. *See* A.N. Jeffares, *Yeats : Man and the Poet,* 229, also his *Introduction to the Poems of W. B. Yeats,* XV and A.G. Stock, W.B. Yeats: *His Poetry and Thought,* 50-51.
17. Inscribed by Yeats on a copy of *The Countess Cathleen.* Quoted by Jim Steward *Eight Modern Writers* (London: OUP), 304.
18. *Autobiographies,* 320-21.
19. *Essays and Introductions,* 148.
20. *Ibid.,* 156-57.
21. *Ibid.,* 160.

22. *Ibid.*, 161.
23. *Collected Poems*, "Notes," 526-27.
24. A.N. Jeffares, *W.B. Yeats: Man and the Poet,* 115.
25. *Autobiographies*, 254.
26. *Ibid.*, 254.
27. C.M. Bowra, *The Heritage of Symbolism*, 193.
28. J. Hone, *W.B. Yeats 1865-1939*, 145-76 and A.N. Jeffares *W.B. Yeats: Man and the Poet*, 115.
29. *Autobiographies*, 353.
30. *Ibid.*, 154.
31. A.N. Jeffares, *W.B. Yeats: Man and the Poet,* 116.
32. Quoted by R. Fallis, *The Irish Renaissance*, 87.
33. Richard Fallis, *The Irish Renaissance,* 89.
34. *Collected Plays*, 50.
35. R. Fallis, *The Irish Renaissance*, 94.
36. A.N. Jeffares, *W.B. Yeats: Man and the Poet,* 139.
37. *Collected Plays*, 18.
38. *Ibid.*, 19.
39. *Autobiographies,* 450-51.
40. Stephen Gwynn, *Irish Literature and Drama*, 158.
41. *Explorations*, 111.
42. *Ibid.*, 229.
43. E. Mikail, ed., *W.B. Yeats: Interviews and Recollections*, (London: Macmillan, 1977), 61.
44. *Uncollected Prose*, Vol. II, 402.
45. *Ibid.*, 402-03.
46. Lennox Robinson, As a Man of Theatre, *W.B. Yeats: Interviews and Recollections*, 256.
47. R. Fallis, *The Irish Renaissance*, 115.
48. *Autobiographies*, 434.
49. *Ibid.*, 435.

4

TOWARDS ARISTOCRACY

I

Variability in politics and encounters at the Abbey prompted Yeats to look for an enduring ideal, an ideal that would provide him order in the world of confusion and instability. Aristocracy gave him all that he immediately needed—defence of his poetry and plays against clerical criticism and popular propagandist verse, strength to fight for the Abbey Theatre and the playwrights against the tutored mob and the anti-Parnellites, and patronage of a sympathiser to encourage him in his creative activities.

In Ireland, as it has been in India, it was aristocracy that always took the lead to overthrow the British rule till the last quarter of the nineteenth century. Naturally, the aristocratic virtues were supreme for the Irish people. Although the Irish society was clearly divided into aristocracy and peasantry, the class conflict was little known and the conflicts which took place between the landlords and the tenants in the late seventies and the early eighties were of little significance. All the nationalists, whatever class they came from, adored Wolfe Tone, Robert Emmet and William Fitzgerald. It was natural for Yeats to take inspiration from the Irish heroes and follow their aristocratic virtues. Lady Gregory's support solidified Yeats's love of aristocracy and aristocratic virtues.

While he was consulting the magical symbols for his future plan, he received the advice from a symbolic personality, who called herself Megarithma, to "live near water and avoid woods because they concentrate the solar ray."[1] He interpreted this enigmatic message that he was advised by his Daimon to fill his imagination with country stories and popular tradition:

> I believed that this enigmatic sentence came from my own Daimon, my own buried self-speaking through my friend's mind. 'Solar,' according to all that I learnt from Mathers, meant elaborate, full of artifice, rich, all that resembles the work of a goldsmith, whereas 'water' meant 'lunar' and 'lunar' all that is simple, popular, traditional, emotional. But why should woods concentrate the solar ray? I did not understand why, nor do I know now, and I decided to reject that part of the message as an error. I accepted the rest without difficulty, for after *The Wanderings of Oisin,* I had simplified my style by filling my imagination with country stories.[2]

A couple of weeks after the message, Lady Gregory, now intimate to Yeats, drove him to Tulira. He stayed at Coole where there was a forest, called the Seven Woods, beside the lake. Advised by his Daimon, Yeats decided to stay at Coole. Probably, the greatest influence on him during the period 1898-1910 was that of Lady Gregory whose care, sympathy and patronage gave him a new life for, at that time, he was in poor health, exhausted by bitter experiences in politics and frustration in love.* She advised Yeats to divert his mind from the bitter memories and brought him from cottage to cottage to gather folk-tales, fairy stories, legends and heroic sagas. She invited him to visit Coole again at the time of his departure.

Widow of Sir William Gregory, a former Governor of Ceylon, Lady Gregory was a plainly dressed woman of forty-eight when Yeats met her for the first time in 1897. She had given up her London house after Sir Williams's death and devoted herself to her son, Robert Gregory, and her estate. She had little knowledge of the conflict between the landlords and the tenants in the late eighteen-seventies and early eighties as she was far away from Ireland during that period. After her final return to Ireland, she maintained the old relationship with her tenants. Yeats writes about her:

---

* I must have spent the summer of 1897 at Coole. I was involved in a miserable love affair, that had but for one brief interruption absorbed my thoughts for years past, and would for some years yet." *Autobiographies*, 399.

> She knew Ireland always in its permanent relationships, associations—violence but a brief interruption—, never lost her sense of feudal responsibility, not of duty as the word is generally understood, but of burdens laid upon her by her station and her character, a choice constantly renewed in solitude.[3]

He quotes an old man to prove how popular she was among her people:

> 'She has been,' said an old man to me, 'like a serving-maid among us. She is plain and simple, like the Mother of God, and that was the greatest lady that ever lived.'[4]

There is no need to repeat her contribution to the Irish dramatic movement which is of first importance; what is equally significant in her patronage of Yeats. Well-versed in Gaelic (she had learnt Gaelic to teach her son the language), she was equally conversant with the peasant dialect and advised Yeats to study their life and language seriously. Besides she collaborated with Yeats in the composition of *Cathleen-ni-Houlihan.* He was always welcome at Coole and in course of time the place became his home. In *Autobiographies* Yeats recollects his stay there:

> Certain woods at Sligo, the woods above Dooney Rock and those above the waterfall at Ben Bulben, though I shall never perhaps walk there again, are so deep in my affections that I dream them at night; and yet the woods at Coole, they do not come into my dream, are so much more knitted to my thoughts that when I am dead they will have, I am persuaded, my longest visit.[5]

A long vista of trees over an undergrowth of clipped laurels, swans at the lake and the clear autumn sky always remained vivid and fresh in his memory. How deeply Yeats loved this place is evident from the poems "The Wild Swans at Coole" and "Coole Park." The first poem vividly paints the sense impressions:

> The trees are in their autumn beauty
> The Woodland paths are dry.
> Under the October twilight water
> Mirrors a still sky
> Upon the brimming water among the stones
> Are nine-and-fifty swans. (*C.P.* 147)

The second poem "Coole Park 1929" is the remembrance of the days of literary activities of the group which he, in co-ordination with Lady Gregory, led successfully:

I meditate upon a swallow's flight,
Upon an aged woman and her house.
A sycamore and line-tree lost in night
Although that western cloud is luminous,
Great works constructed there in nature's spite
For scholars and for poets after us,
Thoughts long knitted into a single thought
A dance-like glory that those walls begot. (*C.P.* 273-74)

Lady Gregory's house at Coole was important for Yeats not only for its scenic beauty and warm hospitality but also because it was the centre of literary activities, activities aimed at Ireland's cultural unity:

There Hyde before he had beaten into prose
That noble blade the Muses buckled on,
There one that ruffled in a manly pose
For all his timid heart, there that slow man,
That meditative man, John Synge, and those
Impetuous men, Shawe-Taylor and Hugh Lane,
Found pride established in humanity,
A scene well set and excellent company. (*C.P.* 274)

In the concluding stanza he pays a rich tribute to Lady Gregory and Coole:

Here, traveller, scholar, poet, take your stand
When all those rooms and passages are gone,
When nettles wave upon a shapeless mound
And saplings root among the broken stone,
And delicate—eyes bent upon the ground,
Back turned upon the bright of the sun
And all the sensuality of the shade—
A moment's memory to that laurelled head. (*C.P.* 274-75)

In "Coole Park And Ballylee, 1931" he remembers the collaboration between him and Lady Gregory how they defended the Irish tradition. The title of the poem significantly refers to the ancient house of Lady Gregory and Yeats's house, Thoor Ballylee, a tower, both symbols of aristocracy and its tradition:

"We were the last romantics—chose for theme
Traditional sanctity and loveliness;
Whatever's written in what poet's name
The book of the people; whatever most can bless
The mind of man or elevate a rhyme; (*C.P.* 276)

He is sad that everything has changed with the dismantling of her house at Coole:

But all is changed, that high horse riderless,
Though mounted in that saddle Homer rode
Where the swan drifts upon a darkening flood. (*C.P.* 276)

Yeats found in aristocracy not only an enduring ideal but also a fort from where he could fight against the anti-Parnellites. Earlier under William Morris's influence he became something of a socialist but the agitation of people tutored by the anti-Parnellite leaders and Lady Gregory's patronage protecting from the onslaught made him an admirer of aristocracy and aristocratic virtues: heroism, nobility, sweetness, love of poetry and fine arts and national pride. He sincerely felt that a perfect relationship between aristocracy and peasantry had to be established (the kind of relationship between Lady Gregory and her people) for the revival of Ireland's old glory.

In the poem "In The Seven Woods" written just after Edward VII's coronation he describes the solace he received at Coole:

I have heard the pigeons of the Seven Woods
Make their faint thunder, and the garden bees
Hum in the lime-tree flowers; and put away
The unavailing outcries and the old bitterness
That empty the heart. (*C.P.* 85)

Next he tells that he has also forgotten the painful humiliation of Ireland and the recent coronation of King Edward VII, marked by the jubilation celebrated in Dublin and other places:

I have forgot awhile
Tara uprooted, and new commonness
Upon the throne and crying about the streets
And hanging its paper flowers from post to post,
Because it is alone of all things happy. (*C.P.* 85)

The solace at Coole has given him strength enough to see beyond the present:

I am contended, for I know that Quiet
Wanders laughing and eating her wild heart
Among pigeons and bees, while that Great Archer
Who but awaits His hour to shoot, still hangs
A cloudy quiver over Pair-na-lee. (*C.P.* 83)

This summary of the poem robs it of its poetic beauty and richness of meaning. Although Yeats sticks to the fourteen lines (of the sonnet form), he breaks the convention in many ways. The first five lines do not express only one feeling or idea. There is the juxtaposition of the contrasting feelings, one aroused by the sweet music of pigeons and bees and the other by the "unavailing outcries and the old bitterness." In the next four lines forgetfulness is not complete, although the poet asserts it to be so; the fall of Tara, former seat of the High Kings and the coronation of Edward VII make him painfully aware of Ireland's slavery. The solace comes, rather weakly after the vision of the Archer at Pair-na-lee. The other feature of the poem is that in his early poetry the cause of grief is something vague, mysterious and far off but here it is real and quotidian.

Yeats visited Italy in 1907. There he happened to read Castiliogne's *The Courtier,* a book about the virtues of aristocracy. His biographer, J. Hone, writes:

> The tour helped to give a further aristocratic turn to Yeats's mind, and he came home to lecture at the National Literary Society on the 'immoral bourgeoisie' without discipline, to which Ireland was surrending her soul.[6]

Now the question arises: how many books on political philosophy did Yeats read to formulate his ideas on the forms of government? The answer will be that he read very few books on the subject. In his time only Plato, Aristotle, Machiavelli, Hobbes, Locke and Rousseau were available and it is unlikely that he had access to modern books on political science. Besides, he hated England from the core of his heart and since that country had begun to be controlled by the middle class, he did not like the idea that Ireland should follow the British system. And the anti-Parnellite group, led by the business class, further accentuated his prejudice against the bourgeoisie. The past history and the contemporary Irish situation made him look to the aristocratic virtues as his ideal. It was a time when the middle class was rising in Ireland and the aristocracy was declining. It is the course of history that whenever there is a conflict between aristocracy and bourgeoisie, either of the two takes the support of the working class, peasantry or serf or protelariat. Yeats, because he favoured aristocracy and hated the middle class, wanted unconsciously a good relationship between the aristocracy and the peasantry of Ireland. The only thing that saved him was his nationalism, humanitarianism and the benevolent character of Lady Gregory. For him, aristocracy meant the rule of the best as Plato and Aristotle conceived it. He believed that the golden period of Ireland was the eighteenth century when the aristocrats and the peasants lived in peaceful harmony and when art and culture flourished without inhibition. For him the Irish tradition was created by aristocracy, peasantry and artists. In the article "Poetry and Tradition,"written in 1907, he laid emphasis on the unity of these three for the continuation and progress of art and culture:

> Three types of men have made all beautiful things; Aristocracies have made beautiful manners, because their place in the world puts them above the fear of life and the countrymen have made beautiful stories and beliefs, because they have nothing to lose and so do not fear, and the artists have made all the rest, because Providence has filled them with recklessness. All these look forward to long tradition, for, being without fear, they have held to whatever pleased them.[7]

He praised the Gore-Booth sisters for their beauty, courtesy and sweetness of manner in the poem "In Memory of Eva Gore-Booth and Con Markiewiez" and lamented Con Markiewicz's mixing with the crowd. In the same spirit he described the aristocratic virtues of Lady Mabel Beardsley in the long poem "Upon a Dying Lady." The opening lines depict the grace on her face at the time of death:

> With the old kindness, the old distinguished grace
> She lies, her lovely piteous head amid dull red hair
> Propped upon pillows, rouge on the pallor of her face.
>
> (*C.P.* 177)

The whole poem is a praise of her race, courage, nobility and generosity. In contrast to aristocracy bourgeoisie was mean, materialistic and enemy of art and culture. Yeats named the Irish bourgeoisie as "merchant" and "the new rich class." He criticised the middle class for its mediocrity and lack of heroic virtues in the article "Poetry and Tradition":

> I could not foresee that a new class, which had begun to rise into power under the shadow of Parnell, would change the nature of the Irish movement, which, needing no longer great sacrifices, nor bringing and great risk to individuals, could do without exceptional men, and those activities of the mind that are founded on the exceptional moment.[8]

Yeats's scorn for the middle class began under John O'Leary's influence:

> A small political organizer told me that he and a certain friend got together somewhere in Tipperary a great meeting of farmers for O'Leary on his coming out of prison, and O'Leary had said at it: 'The landlords gave us some few leaders, and I like them for that, and the artisans have given us great numbers of good patriots, and so I like them best; but you I do not like at all, for you have never given us any one.[9]

II

The year 1897 marked the beginning of a new era in Yeats's political career. As described earlier, Parnell's tragic death and betrayal of a large number of the Irish people left Yeats stunned. The conflict that ensued between the Parnellites and the anti-Parnellites proved to be the thin end of the wedge in Irish politics. However, Yeats recovered his strength soon and, inspite of the upper hand of the anti-Parnellites, maintained his optimism and trust in the heroic qualities of aristocracy. The "Red Hanrahan's Song" expresses his optimism. The poem opens with the description of the storm (political) sweeping over the country and creating havoc:

> The old brown-trees break into two over Cummen Strand
> Under a bitter black wind that blows from the left hand,
> Our courage breaks like an old tree in a black wind
> and dies. (*C.P.* 90)

We know that "tree" is one of the complex symbols of Yeats; it stands for life in "The Two Trees" and for Ireland in "Dedication to a Book of Stories Selected from the Irish Novelists." It stands for old Ireland as it is both "old" and "brown." "The black wind that blows from the left hand" is the political wind created by England, (if we stand in the northern part of Ireland and face Dublin, England will be on the left side), which is wrecking the entire nation. Set against this political turmoil is the poet's determination to keep the fire of nationalism burning:

> But we have hidden in our hearts the flame
> out of the eyes
> Of Cathleen, the daughter of Houlihan.

This feeling of nationalism is reiterated through a set of images in the second stanza:

> The wind has bundled up the clouds high over Knocknarea,
> And thrown the thunder on the shore for all that Maeve
> can say.
> Angers that are like noisy clouds have set our hearts abeat
> But we have all bent low and kissed the quiet feet
> Of Cathleen the daughter of Houlihan. (*C.P.* 98)

With the hope that whatever calamities may come, there will be triumph of Ireland ultimately, the poem ends with a prophetic note:

> The yellow pool has overflowed high up on
> Clooth-na-Bare.
> For the wet winds are blowing out of the clinging air;
> Like heavy flooded waters our bodies and our blood;
> But purer than a candle before the Holy Rood
> Is Cathleen, the daughter of Houlihan. (*C.P.* 99)

What is remarkable of this poem is its artistic quality. No doubt, it is aglow with patriotism, but it outlives its time for its rich music, experimental rhythm and fitting imagery. The metre and rhythm remind us of Whitman and the whole poem is a metaphor; the pure bright flame of nationalism goes on burning at the feet of *Cathleen-ni-Houlihan* against the roaring wind, dark clouds and black rain.

This optimism was further strengthened by the Wyndham Land Act of 1903. The Act enacted by the British government with the support of the Unionists that forced the Irish landlords to sell their estates to their tenants if three-quarters of the tenants wished to buy them. The socialist leader Horace Plunkett, who had worked hard for establishing agricultural co-operatives, welcomed this revolutionary act. George Russell (A.E.), on Yeats's advice, joined the co-operative movement. This reform, although admirable and beneficent for the small farmers, could not attract people much because they wanted freedom first and land reform later. Richard Fallis comments on the failure of co-operatives:

> Valuable as they were, even these reforms were little too late in terms of satisfying Irish people with British rule. Despite the national humiliation of the fall of Parnell and its aftermath, the sense of Irish nationalism continued to rise. The Irish politicians squabbled and made themselves ineffectual but the people developed almost daily their sense of Irish self-identity.[10]

Yeats, after first enthusiasm, got disillusioned with the British government's plan of land reform, although he continued to support Plunkett's co-operative movement. The main reason for his disillusionment was that he found that the land reform act had failed to achieve the goal for which it was enacted and related to it was the break of the good old relationship between the aristocrats and the peasants of the country. The poem "Upon a House Shaken By The Land Agitation" is an expression of his ambivalent attitude towards land reform and its consequences. The prose draft explains his intention in the poem:

> How should the world gain, if this house failed, even though a hundred little houses were better for it; for here power has given poetry or legend, giving energy, precision, and it gave to a far people beneficial rule, and still under its roof the living intellect is sweetened by old memories of its descent from far off. How should the world be better if the wren's nest flourish and the Eagle's house be shattered.[11]

This idea, the grief at the destruction of aristocratic houses, centres of culture and art, is expressed artistically in the poem:

How should the world be luckier if this house
Where passion and precision have been one
Times out of mind, became too ruinous
To breed the lidless eye that loves the sun. (*C.P.* 106)

Here he does not regret the material loss; all that he is worried about is the loss of the noble qualities of aristocracy, symbolised by the eagle "the lidless eye that loves the sun," heroism, passion, courage and subjectivity exhibited by the Irish heroes in the past.

The poem "These Are The Clouds" is a consolation to Lady Gregory, indirectly to the poet also, that the value of her work and the principles she has stood by are assured. The aristocratic majesty is beautifully compared to the fallen sun surrounded by clouds which enhance its tragic majesty:

And therefore, friend, if your great race were run
And these things came, so much the more thereby
Have you made greatness your companion
Although it be for children that you sigh:
These are the clouds about the fallen sun
The majesty that shuts his burning eyes. (*C.P.* 108)

These two poems on Lady Gregory combine the public and personal experiences in a rare way; the complex symbols and images transcend the limits of politics and give them permanence.

The second reason for Yeats's disenchantment with land reform was his apprehension that the movement launched by Dr. Hyde would come to a halt if the schism between aristocracy and peasantry was allowed by land agitation to go wider; for, to him, the aristocratic class was the patron of art and poetry and symbol of the rich Irish tradition and if there was a conflict between the aristocracy and the peasantry the unity of Ireland and the harmony in society would break for ever. The essays "Poetry and Tradition" and "Synge and the Ireland of His Time" give us a good idea of his mind's working during the period 1903-10. In the first essay, he explains the reason why he absented himself from O'Leary's funeral:

When O'Leary died, I could not bring myself go to his funeral, though I had been once his close fellow-worker,

> for I shrank from seeing about his grave so many whose nationalism was different from anything he had thought or that I could share.[12]

What was Yeats's ideal then? The answer is there in the essay:

> I, on the other hand, was more preoccupied with Ireland... and took from Allingham and Walsh their passion for country spiritism, and from Ferguson his pleasure in heroic legend, and while seeing all in the light of European literature found my symbols of expression in Ireland. One thought, often possessed me strongly. Now from the influence, mainly the personal influence of William Morris, I dreamed enlarging hate, till we had come to hate with a passion of patriotism what Morries and Ruskin hated.... A new belief seemed coming that could be so simple and demonstrable and above all so mixed into common scenery of the world, that it would set the whole man on fire and liberate him from a thousand obediences and complexities. We were to forge in Ireland a new sword on our old traditional anvil for that great battle that must in the end re-establish the old, confident joyous world.... All who have any old traditions have something of aristocracy, but we had opposing us from the first, though not strongly from the first, a type of mind which had been without it in that of Davis, and which has made a new nation out of Ireland that was once old and full of memories.[13]

This ideal of reviving old romantic Ireland was cherished by all the Irish nationalists. What was the need of the time was to make effort for it by all means. Yeats chose the most important means, literature, for the purpose. Earlier he had predicted in the article "Nationalism and Literature" that after poetry was the coming of drama. He, therefore, launched the project, Irish dramatic movement, which proved, later on, to be the greatest movement with far reaching effects in the first half of the twentieth century. As described earlier, the experiences of the movement were bitter-sweet. The orthodox criticised the *Countess Cathleen* and the prude *Playboy of the Western World.* On the other hand *Cathleen-ni-Houlihan, The Rising of the Moon, Riders to the Sea, Deirdre* and *Diarmid* and Grania attracted large crowds and were applauded greatly all over Ireland.

The Abbey Theatre experiences made Yeats more realistic. He began to realise the fact that uniting Ireland by means of literature was a more difficult task than he had thought of and that he had to define his own position and choose whether he should be a poet or an active politician. He chose, and rightly so, to be a poet. However, it was a wrong decision to resign from the IRB under Maud Gonne's influence. Love makes people fool but it made Yeats more. Later on he realized his mistake and took the mantle of a *fili.*

Jon Stallworthy, quoting Eleanor Knott's distinction between the bard and the *fili* made in her book *Irish Classical Poetry,* points out that Yeats assumed the role of the *fili.* The bard, according to Knott, is simply a poet and versifier, and the *fili* is a poet and guardian of the traditional knowledge:

> According to the early metrical tracts the bard is simply a poet and versifier; the fili is a poet, a scholar and guardian of traditional knowledge; he is especially a prophet and a seer and can wield supernatural powers. In short, he somewhat resembles in his functions the druid of pre-Christian Gaul.

The volume *Responsibilities,* as John Unterecker has pointed out[13], consists of supernatural, social, personal and aesthetic responsibilities. Nobody can deny his conclusion; but if we follow Stallworthy and Knott we can more precisely say that all these responsibilities are of an Irish *fili.*

"The Grey Rock" the first poem of the volume defines Yeats's position as a *fili* of Ireland. It is closely related to "All Things Can Tempt Me" where he regrets his obsession with the politics of his country and love of Maud Gonne which deviated him from the true path of poetry:

> All things can tempt me from this craft of verse:
> One time it was a woman's face, or worse—
> The seeming needs of my fool-driven land. (*C.P.* 109)

In "The Grey Rock" he elaborates the theme,— his responsibility as a poet, by means of an allegory. He invokes the dead poets of Rhymer's club with whom he learnt his trade. Those poets never made a compromise in their defence of poetry:

You kept the Muse's sterner laws,
And unrepenting faced your ends
And therefore earned the right.... (*C.P.* 117)

Side by side goes the story of Aoife and her distress. She lodges a complaint against her lover, a poet, who is dead now. She narrates before the Gods the sorrowful state of her love that her lover, an Irishman, supported his king in the battle between him and the Danes. As she had bestowed immortality on him for two hundred, she gave him a pin that could make him invisible. He drove away the Danes by his shouts:

When this day
Murrough, the king of Ireland son,
Foot after foot was giving war,
He and his best troops back to back,
Had perished there, but the Danes ran
Stricken with panic from the attack,
The shouting of an unseen man. (*C.P.* 117)

But the sight of the wounded king moved him deeply. He forgot Aoife's words, threw down the pin and fought physically with the enemies. As he became visible, the Danes located him easily and killed him. The allegorical meaning is that Aoife is the goddess of poetry and her lover is a poet. The pin, her gift, is the poetical talent which makes him an invisible warrior, a warrior who does not fight in the battlefield but encourages his people by his words. But if he discards the "pin" and does not follow the sterner laws of poetry, the Goddess of poetry is aggrieved. But when she expresses her anger before the Gods, they smile and drench her with wine to make her happy:

But thereon every god stood up
With a slow smile and without sound,
And stretching forth his arm and cup
To where she moaned upon the mound,
Suddenly drenched her to the skin;
And she with Goban's wine adrip,
No more remembering what had been
Stared at the gods with laughing lip. (*C.P.* 119)

It means that the Gods support the poet's action. Mere aestheticism is not sufficient. A poet must be faithful to his country and for that be ready to sacrifice his life.

The lines printed in italics, addressed to the poets of the Rhymers' club defend his stance. His countrymen demand from him active participation in current politics but his friends expect him to follow the Muse's sterner laws. Yeats combines the two; he cannot ignore either. In the concluding stanza where both the stories unite, Yeats defines his position:

I have kept my faith, though faith was tried,
To that rock-born, rock-wandering foot,
And the world's altered since you died.
And I am in no good repute
With the loud host before the sea,
That think sword-strokes were better meant
Than lover's music—let that be,
So that the wandering foot's content. (*C.P.* 119)

Yeats's position is clear; he cannot blindly follow his friends' principle of art for art's sake nor take arms in his hand to fight straight. The best course for him is to combine the two together, poetry and politics.

The poem entitled "Introductory Rhymes" is the other side of his views on the responsibilities of a poet. He counts the heroic men of his family—the Dublin merchant, the country scholar, the soldier, the butler and "the old merchant skipper that leaped overboard/After a ragged hat in Biscay Bay." He regrets that he has no heir to continue the tradition of his family. How can a poet be audacious enough to write a poem on his family line? Perhaps, Yeats's intention is not to praise the notable figures of his family but to trace the elements of heroism in his blood and grieve at his failure at passing them over to the next generation:

Although I have come close on fortynine,
I have no child, I have nothing but a book
Nothing but that to prove your blood and mine.
(*C.P.* 113)

The only thing he has to offter is a book of poems to his dead forefathers and his countrymen.

The important poems in *Responsibilities* illustrate Yeats's view point of combining politics and poetry. The poems "September 1913," "To a Wealthy Man" and "To A Friend" were written during the period of controversy over the Hugh Lane pictures. In the controversy Yeats saw a threat to art and poetry, the means by which the unity of culture could be established in Ireland. He had already faced the trouble over the staging of *Countess Cathleen* and *The Playboy of the Western World*. Indignant at the lack of understanding the powerful drama *The Playboy* by a section of his people he wrote the short satirical poem "On Those That Hated the Playboy of the Western World":

> Once, when midnight smote the air,
> Eunuchs ran through Hell and met
> On every crowded street to stare
> Upon great Juan riding by.
> Even like those to rail and sweat
> Staring upon his sinewy thigh. (*C.P.* 124)

A passage entered in the *Diary* kept in 1909 gives a good idea of the poem's background:

> The root of it all is that the political class in Ireland—the lower-middle class from whom the patriotic associations have drawn their journalists and their leaders for the last ten years—have suffered through the cultivation of hatred as the one energy of their movement, a deprivation which is the intellectual equivalent to a certain surgical operation. Hence the shrillness of their voices. They contemplate all creative power as the eunuchs contemplate Don Juan as he passes through Hell on the white horse.[14]

"An Appointment" is a beautiful short poem written on the injustice done to Hugh Lane. He was denied the post of the curator of the Dublin Museum by Lord Aberdeen and Augustus Birrel, then, Chief Secretary of Ireland. Yeats begins the poem in a mood of disappointment:

> Being out of heart with government
> I took a broken root to fling
> Where the proud, wayward squirrel went
> Taking delight that he could spring. (*C.P.* 141)

The contrast between the dejected poet and the "wayward squirrel" is significant, besides the "broken root." The poet throws the broken root with the intention of surprising the squirrel; but the result is different. The expected delight is changed into a different kind of delight. He realises the truth that those who have freer spirit and mind do not think of favour nor are they ruffled by the kind of treatment that was given to Sir Hugh Lane:

> Nor the tame will, nor timid brain
> Nor heavy knitting of the brow
> Bred that fierce tooth and cleanly limb.
> And threw him up to laugh on the bough
> No government appointed him. (*C.P.* 141)

Both the poems are a prelude to the poems written on the controversy of the Hugh Lane pictures. The main target of Yeats's attack is the middle class led by the anti-Parnellites, Martin Murphy and Tim Healy. According to Joseph Hone Murphy and Healy were not particularly closely associated with the Land League but they actively participated in the religious, communal, economic and social activities of the boycott. After Parnell's divorce case the "Sullivan gang," under the leadership of Healy and Murphy attacked Parnell on ethical grounds and thus incurred the displeasure of Yeats.[15] But Hone's account does not complete the picture; Yeats's hostility to Murphy and Healy increased when he found that they were instigating the other factory owners to exploit their factory workers who were avowedly left. The workers' leaders, James Connolly, one of the heroes of the Easter Rising, and James Larkin, firmly believed that the cause of Irish nationalism was basically an economic question. They tried hard to organise the workers through their organisation, the Irish Transport and General Workers' Union. Richard Fallis has accurately and objectively described the workers' condition at that time and James Connolly's and James Larkin's ideas and programme of action:

> A largely independent Ireland which still permitted one class to exploit another would be free in name only, he [Connolly] believed, and he worked for the day when Ireland would become a socialist republic. In the meantime, there was organising to be done in the slums and factories of Dublin and Belfast, for workers in both cities, too, lived in the midst of terrible economic exploitation.... More than half the population of Dublin was sporadically

> employed or out of work; for those with jobs, ninety-hour work weeks were not uncommon. There was a great task for the unions to do, and Connolly and Larkin threw themselves into it.[16]

Martin Murphy, Tim Healy and other employers could not tolerate the workers' demand for better living. They declared lockout in the year 1913 and threw out 24000 workers out of job. What followed after the lockout were strikes, starvation and police brutality. The Catholic clergy opposed the plan to send children to England for the winter to avoid starvation on the plea that they would be converted to the religion of the Protestant England. Yeats could not tolerate the callousness of Murphy, Healy and the Catholic Church. He criticised the police, the press and the clergy in a letter which was published in the *Irish Worker* 1913. The letter is quoted in full for a full understanding of his feelings and point of view:

> I do not complain of Dublin's capacity for fanaticism whether in priest or layman, for you cannot have strong feeling without that capacity, but neither those who directed the police nor the editors of our newspaper can plead fanaticism. They are supposed to watch over our civil liberties, and I charge the Dublin Nationalist newspapers with deliberately arousing religious passion to break up the organisation of the working men, with appealing to mob law day after day, with publishing the names of working men and their wives for purposes of intimidation.
>
> And I charge the Unionist Press of Dublin and those who directed the police with conniving at this conspiracy. I want to know why the *Daily Express* which is directly and indirectly inciting Ulster to rebellion in defence of what it calls "the liberty of the subject" is so indifferent to that liberty here in Dublin that it has not made one editorial comment, and I ask the *Irish Times* why a few sentences at the end of an article, too late in the week to be of any service, has been the measure of its love for civil liberty?
>
> I want to know why there were only (according to the Press reports) two policemen at King's Bridge on Saturday when Mr. Sheely Skeffington was assaulted and a man

> prevented from buying a ticket for his own child? There had been tumults every night at every Dublin station, and I can only assume that the police authorities wish those tumults to continue.
>
> I want to know why the mob at North Wall and elsewhere were permitted to drag children from their parents' arms, and by what right one woman was compelled to open her box and show a marriage certificate; I want to know by what right the police have refused to accept charges against rioters; I want to know who has ordered the abrogation of the most elementary rights of the citizens, and why authorities who are bound to protect everyman in doing that which he has a legal right to do—even though they have to call upon all the forces of the Crown—have permitted the Ancient Order of Hibernians to besiege Dublin, taking possession of the railway stations like a foreign army.

Prime Minister has fallen and Ministers of State have been impeached for less than this. I demand that the coming Police Inquiry shall be so widened that we may get to the bottom of a conspiracy, whose like has not been seen in any English-speaking town during living memory. Intriguers have met together somewhere behind the scene that they might turn the religion of Him who thought it hard for a rich man to enter into the kingdom of Heaven into (sic) an oppression of the poor.[17]

Commenting on the letter Conor Cruise O'Brien remarks:

> The events of the Dublin Lock-out including the events which Yeats described aroused strong emotions and there can be no doubt that Yeats's indignation was genuine and that it sprang, in part, from those human feelings which we find them inconvenient, we call "humanitarian zeal.[18]

O'Brien's long paper "Passion and Cunning: Yeats's Politics," although brilliant and highly logical, does not do justice to the poet. The main aim of the learned writer is to prove that Yeats was an opportunist politician who regulated his passion in poetry to achieve political gains. It is difficult to agree with the view that Yeats was a calculative politician who watched the opportune time to write or publish his political poems. The phrase humanitarian zeal is placed within quotation marks in the article to mean that Yeats wrote the letter at an opportune time to cash the feelings of the labourers and malign the image of his political opponents. O'Brien is prejudiced against Yeats. Yeats was always against abstraction and calculation; he never went against the poor working people and always pleaded for a unity between the peasants and their landlords. Besides, Yeats was a humanitarian from the core of his heart and never planned to exploit the common man for his personal gains. In fact, O'Brien has carried his prejudice too far and failed to see the "real" Yeats; he must have considered the poems on the Easter Rising in which the ordinary men who were earlier insignificant in Yeats's eyes are made great heroes. If Yeats's letter does not fit in the framework as designed by O'Brien, how do the Easter Rising, and the Civil War poems and *Cathleen-ni-Houlihan, Countess Cathleen* and *The Unicorn from the Star* fit in that frame? He must be aware of the fact that genuine feelings do not spring from opportunism. Yeats was never a propagandist in the sense O'Brien estimates him and the charge that Yeats's love of aristocracy made him a ruthless man is off the point because Yeats always believed in heroic virtues and his ideal was Sir Philip Sidney who allowed his soldier to drink the water which was brought for him when he was badly injured in the battlefield. Patrick Cosgrave very rightly refutes O'Brien's arguments:

> It is my belief that his approach to Yeats is, in fact, the reverse of historical; that while his apparent ignorance of Yeats's poetics disqualified him from his undertaking before the start, it is primarily as a narrator of fact that he is found wanting.... There is, in fact, no evidence whatever to suggest that Yeats's motives for writing the letter were other than the humanitarian ones stated in it.[19]

After the Dublin Lockout came the controversy over the site of the gallery for Sir Hugh Lane's collection of rare modern French pictures. Hugh Lane wanted the pictures to be suitably housed by the Corporation. His demand for the bridge site across the Liffey river met with popular opposition. Lane's chief critic was the *Independent* of which Martin Murphy was the proprietor, Yeats's old enemy. J. Hone writes:

> Yeats chose to regard Martin Murphy a man of distinct character and appearance, to whose energy in Industrial enterprise Dublin was under considerable debt, as a representative type of the middle class which had begun to rise into power under the shadow of the Land League and kindred agitations. This Murphy certainly was not, even though he was ignorant of art and allowed his newspaper too much latitude in abuse.[20]

Here J. Hone is defensive of Murphy and this is because he lacks Yeats's sensitivity, perhaps. Yeats was a great mind. He could and did react against events and people with full force but soon would detach himself from the scene and meditate calmly over his reaction and philosophise the entire issue. The different events, political or politically inspired, made him believe that the Irish middle class led by Martin Murphy and Tim Healy was inimical to his plan of reviving the unity of culture by means of literature. He stated his point of view explicitly in the "Notes" to the poems written in the period 1913-15:

> In the thirty years or so during which I have been reading Irish newspaper, three public controversies have stirred my imagination. The first was the Parnell controversy. There were reasons to justify a man's joining either party, but there were none to justify, on one side or on the other, lying accusations forgetful of past services, a frenzy of detraction. And another was the dispute over the *Playboy*. There may have been reasons for opposing as for supporting that violent, laughing thing, though I can see the one side only, but there cannot have been any for the lies, for the unscrupulous rhetoric spread against it in Ireland, and from Ireland to America. The third prepared for the corporation's refusal of a building for Sir Hugh Lane's famous collection of pictures.... These controversies, political, literary and artistic have shown that neither religion nor politics can of itself create minds with enough to make a nation.... Religious Ireland—and the pious Protestants of my childhood were signal examples—thinks of divine things as a round of duties separated from life and not as an element that may be discovered in all circumstances and emotion, while political Ireland sees the good citizen but as a man

> who holds to certain opinions and not as a man of good will. Against all this we have but a few educated men and the remnant of an old traditional culture among the poor. Both were stronger forty years ago, before the rise of our new middle class which made its first display during the nine years of the Parnellite split, showing how base at moments of excitement are minds without culture.[21]

The "Notes" make it amply clear that Yeats's purpose in writing poems like "To A Wealthy Man" and "September 1913" was not only to criticise the new middle class but also to show the Irish people the value of culture and art. Yeats's letter to Sir Hugh Lane explains the background of the poem "To A Wealthy Man":

> January, (1913) 18, Woburn Buildings
>
> My dear Lane,
>
> Here is the poem. If it is not politic tell me frankly. If you think it politic I will try and see Hone to see if fitting publication and comment could be made in the *Irish Times.* I have tried to meet the argument in Lady Ardilaun's letter to somebody, her objection to giving because of Home Rule and Lloyd George, and still more to meet the general argument of people like Ardilaun that they should not give unless there is a public demand. I shall quite understand if you think it would be unwise to draw attention to the possible slightness of "Paudeens" (little Patrick) desire for any kind of art. I left Dublin nearly a month ago and have no idea how the fund is or what has occurred. I kept the poem longer than I intended to make some slight changes.
>
> Yours ever
>
> W.B. Yeats[22]

The poem is a request to Lord Ardilaun who had argued that money should not be given unless there was a clear public demand for the project. Yeats's argument here is that there is no need of public consultation when a great and useful work is to be done. He refers to three incidents as described in Castiglione's *The Courtier,* the first is that of Duke Erocle who did not consult the business class to stage the five plays of Plautus:

What cared Duke Erocle, that bid
His mummers to the market-place
What th' onion-sellers thought or did
So that his Plautus set the pace
For the Italian comedies. (*C.P.* 119)

The second reference is to the Duke of Urbino who did not care to take advice from the common people when he made "the grammar school of courtesies."

And Guidaboldo, when he made
That grammar school of courtesies
Where wit and beauty learned their trade
Upon Urbino's windy hill
That he might learn the shepherd's will. (*C.P.* 119-20)

The third example is Cosimo de Medici who ignored the public opinion when he commissioned the architect, Michelozzo, to design St. Mark Library in Florence:

And when they drove out Cosimo,
Indifferent how the rancour ran,
He gave the hours they had set free
To Michelozzo's latest plan
For the San Marco Library. (*C.P.* 120)

At the end Yeats makes a fervent appeal to the perspective donor, Lord Ardilaun, to give up the ways of "Paudeens" and "Biddies" and contribute generously to the project fund for the preservation of art in Ireland:

"Look up in the sun's eye and give
What the exultant heart calls good
That some new day may breed the best
Because you gave, not what they would
But the right twigs for an eagle's nest." (*C.P.* 120)

Martin Murphy understood the hidden satire in the poem and reacted sharply to it. He started a severe and vitriolic attack on Yeats. J. Hone writes about it:

> The Paudeens, however, held the floor; one man compared the pictures to the Trojan horse which destroyed a city,

> and Lane and his friends, rich and poor, were described as "self-seekers," "self-advertisers," "picture-dealers," "roll-logging cranks," and "fanatics."

Yeats's counter-reply, again a poem, was more heated. He abandoned the bland tone of "To A Wealthy Man" in "September 1913" and advised them to multiply their money as they were wont to:

> What need you, being come to sense,
> But fumble in a greasy till
> And add the half pence to the pence
> And prayer to shivering prayer, until
> You have dried the marrow from the bone? (*C.P.* 120-21)

The "Paudeens" are contrasted with the heroic figures of the past:

> Yet they were of a different kind,
> The names that stilled your childish play
> They have gone about the world like wind. (*C.P.* 121)

In an angry and bitter tone Yeats contrasts the low-minded Murphy and his people with the past heroes Edward Fitzgerald, Robert Emmet and Wolfe Tone who gave everything they had for the sake of Ireland:

> "Was it for this the wild geese spread
> The grey wing upon every tide;
> For this that all that blood was shed,
> For this Edward Fitzgerald died,
> And Robert Emmet and Wolfe Tone,
> All that delirium of the brave? (*C.P.* 121)

Yeats is sad and angry at the same time that the modern Irish people are disregarding the noble sacrifice of their ancestors who never thought of multiplying money. The demonstrative pronoun "this" is the most important word in this passage. Repeated three times, it expresses Yeats's anguish over the new rich people's apathetic attitude to the noble and heroic qualities for which Ireland is known. He deliberately uses the word "delirium" to criticise the attitude of Murphy and his people. He speaks in a sad tone:

> Yet could we turn the years again,
> And call those exiles as they were

In all their loneliness and pain,
You'd cry, "Some woman's yellow hair
Has maddened every mother's son';
They weighed so lightly what they gave.
But let them be, they're dead and gone,
They're with O'Leary in the grave. (*C.P.* 121)

The refrain "Romantic Ireland's dead and gone/It's with O'Leary in the grave" that occurs at the end of the first three stanzas becomes clear in the concluding stanza where we learn that Yeats by "romantic" means the opposite of "calculative." We understand that the exiles (O'Leary was one of the last) gave everything (Land and family) but now people are so selfish that they oppose all that is noble and heroic.

"To A Friend" and "Paudeen," as Professor Rajan points out, assert the artist's pride and solitariness against the middle class people. I agree with him but they convey something more than this; they are closely related to September 1913 and "To A Wealthy Man" and defend the position of those people who are defeated by the rancorous clamour of the crowd. "To A Friend" is a consolation to Lady Gregory, suggesting her to keep quiet and not to care for her failure in her attempt to help Sir Hugh Lane because for a lady of her qualities it is difficult to compete with shameless people:

Now all the truth is out
Be secret and take defeat
From any brazen throat
For how can you compete,
Being honour bred.... (*C.P.* 122)

The best thing, therefore, is to accept defeat heroically:

Be secret and exult
Because of all things known
That is most difficult. (*C.P.* 122)

These concluding lines, though meant to console Lady Gregory, console all those who have worked hard for a noble cause but have been thwarted in their endeavour by lumpen elements. For Yeats pride is a virtue if it does not hurt others. George Eliot holds the same view. At the end of Chapter 6 in the *Middlemarch* she reflects:

> We mortals, men and women, devour many a disappointment between breakfast and dinner-time; keep back the tears and look a little pale about the lips, and in answer to inquiries say, 'Oh, nothing!' Pride helps us; and pride is not a bad thing when it only urges to hide our own hurts—not to hurt others.[23]
>
> (*Middlemarch* 52-3)

"Paudeens" is the vision of an artist's triumph. Indignant at the obsçure spite of the Pandeens, the poet stumbles through stones and thorn trees and reaches a high windy place. Thereafter hearing the call of a curlew and the answer of the other, he realizes the coming of a bright morning that will clear all the confusion prevailing. The phrase "a sweet crystalline cry" stands for the artistic creation in the concluding lines and because the Paudeens lack the "crystalline cry," they will have no place in God's kingdom:

> That on the lonely height where all are in God's eye
> There cannot be, confusion of our sound forgot,
> A single soul that lacks a sweet crystalline cry. (*C.P.* 122)

"To A Shade," the last of the series, is a powerful poem. Yeats links the past with the present by means of juxtaposition. The shade is Parnell's ghost, a victim of Tim Healy's criticism. The poet in his address to the ghost says that the town has not changed outwardly since the day of Parnell's death. The beautiful evening sea, the fresh breeze, the flying gulls and the majestic houses will please him but he should not be tricked by this. If the town is not changed, his enemies too are unchanged. The aside in the first stanza tells us the attitude of the Paudeens:

> If you have revisited the town, thin Shade,
> Whether to look upon your monument
> (I wonder if the builder has been paid.) (*C.P.* 123)

In the past it was he who was wronged by Tim Healy; now it is Hugh Lane who is the target of his attack. Lane, like Santa Claus, brought:

> In his full hands what, had they only known
> Had given their children's children loftier thought
> Sweeter emotion, working in their veins
> Like gentle blood. (*C.P.* 123)

But they in their ignorance have ill-treated him.

> He—has been driven from the place,
> And insult heaped upon him for his pains,
> And for his open-handedness, disgrace;
> Your enemy, an old foul mouth, had set
> The pack upon him. (*C.P.* 123)

He advises the shade to go back to its grave because Ireland is still infested with bad people:

> Go unquiet wanderer
> And gather the Glasnevin coverlet
> About your head till the dust stops your ear. (*C.P.* 123)

And finally,

> You had enough of sorrow before death—
> Away, away! You are safer in the tomb. (*C.P.* 123)

These lines reveal Yeats's sympathy for Parnell no doubt, but the underlying irony is a truculent criticism of Murphy and Healy who, in his opinion, are enemies of culture.

The epilogue which closes the volume is linked with the "Introductory Rhymes." Unterecker points out that the poem "A Coat":

> brings the section to a formal end with its announcement that Yeats will henceforth walk naked and the epilogue ("While I, from that reed-throated Whisper") pulls the entire section into organic unity.[24]

Unterecker is right in his conclusion but what he has missed is that the epilogue is Yeats's final turn to aristocracy and he asserts the supremacy of aristocracy and poetry. Tired of the quarrels with the hostile multitude of the middle class (I need not refer to the long passage from the "Notes" I quoted earlier), Yeats took shelter at Coole. Lady Gregory's patronage and friendship with the poets of Rhymers' Club gave him strength to gather his energy. Now he is strong enough to maintain equanimity even if his priceless things are defiled by foul men:

> I can forgive even that wrong of wrongs
> Those undreamt accidents that have made me
> Seeing that Fame has perished this long while
> Being but a part of ancient ceremony—

Notorious, till all my priceless things
Are but a post the passing dogs defile. (*C.P.* 143)

All these four poems—"All Things Tempt Me," "The Grey Rock," the "Introductory Rhymes" and the "Closing Rhymes"—connected thematically to one another, define the nature of Yeats's later poetry. "All Things Tempt Me" conveys Yeats's resolution to keep himself at a distance from Irish politics and Maud Gonne's love; "The Grey Rock" defines his function as a *fili*; the "Introductory Rhymes" expresses his love of the Irish tradition preserved by the ancient families of Ireland and the "Closing Rhymes" defines the stance he is going to take in future. Although he cannot keep aloof from the current Irish politics, he will pull out for sometime to meditate on the happenings and his own action and philosophise the entire chain of actions and events to incorporate them in his system and poetry. The poems of the period 1913-15, all having their source in politics, are the product of meditation at a cool place.

"The Fisherman," written in June 1914 illustrates Yeats's ideal of theme, diction and style of poetry. The fisherman is a representative Irishman but he does not exist in flesh and blood as he is the ideal but is as real as reality can be:

The freckled man who goes
To a grey place on a hill
In grey Connemara clothes
At dawn to cast his flies. (*C.P.* 166)

In the subsequent three lines we come to know that he is a part of Yeats's imagination:

It's long since I began
To call up to the eyes
This wise and simple man. (*C.P.* 166)

He describes his experiences, painful and bitter, in the rest of the lines of the stanza. The second and final stanza again comes back to the vision of the fisherman and tells us of the poet's ideal of poetry. The ideal fisherman is the other side of Yeats and is different from Red Hanrahan, the passionate young man:

Maybe a twelvemonth since
Suddenly I began

In scorn of this audience,
Imagining a man,
. . . . .
A man who does not exist
A man who is but a dream. (*C.P.* 167)

Earlier he had thought of writing poetry "for my own race/And the reality." Now he finds the solution in the fisherman:

Before I am old
I shall have written him one
Poem maybe as cold
And passionate as the dawn. (*C.P.* 167)

"The People" seems on the surface to be the poet's confession of the guilt that he did not give full time to poetry:

I might have used the one substantial right
My trade allows: chosen my company
And chosen what scenery pleased me best. (*C.P.* 169-70)

Maud Gonne reproves him for his complaint and says:

The drunkards, pilferers of public funds,
All the dishonest crowd I had driven away,
When my luck changed and they dared meet my face,
Crawled from obscurity, and set upon me
Those I had served and some that I had fed;
Yet never have I; now nor any time,
Complained of the people. (*C.P.* 170)

Yeats replies weakly:

You that have not lived in thought but deed,
Can have the purity of a natural force,
But I, whose virtues are the definitions
Of the analytic mind nor keep my tongue from speech.
(*C.P.* 170)

Although his reply is convincing but he knows at heart that Maud Gonne's words are substantial and he cannot ignore the common people despite his love of aristocracy and its virtues:

And yet because my heart leaped at her words,
I was abashed, and now they come to mind
After nine years, I sink my head abashed. (*C.P.* 170)

Yeats is definitely an advocate of aristocracy at this stage but his concept of aristocracy is quite different. He is never in favour of despotism, nepotism, exploitation and scorn of the common people. He is in favour of aristocracy for its nobility, virtues, heroism and love of art and culture. It is the conflict between his partisan aristocracy and the love of the common people that makes him vacillate from one side to the other. "The People" reveals this kind of vacillation. His later poetry shows this kind of conflict, tension and vacillation at different planes and attempts to resolve all kinds of antiomy at different levels.

REFERENCES

1. *Autobiographies,* 371.
2. *Ibid.*, 371-72.
3. *Ibid.*, 395.
4. *Ibid.*, 395.
5. *Ibid.*, 377-78.
6. J. Hone, *W.B. Yeats 1865-1939*, 219-20.
7. *Essays and Introductions*, 251.
8. R. Fallis, *The Irish Renaissance*, 74.
9. Quoted by J. Hone, *W.B. Yeats 1865-1939*, 22.
10. *Essays and Introductions*, 246.
11. *Ibid.*, 248-50.
12. Jon Stallworthy, *Vision and Revision in Yeats's Poetry*, 26.
13. J. Unterecker, *A Reader's Guide to W.B. Yeats*, 113-14.
14. *Autobiographies*, 486.
15. J. Hone, *W.B. Yeats 1865-1939*, 265.
16. W.B. Yeats, "Dublin Fanaticism," *Irish Worker*, November, 1913. Quoted by C.C.O' Brien "Passion and Cunning," *In Excited Reverie*, 230-31.
17. *Ibid.*, 231-32.
18. Patrick Cosgrave, "Yeats, Fascism and Conor O'Brien," *London Magazine*, July 1967, Vol. 7, 22-41.
19. J. Hone, *W.B. Yeats 1865-1939*, 265.
20. *Collected Poems*, "Notes," 529-30.
21. A. Wade, ed., *The Letters of W.B. Yeats*, 573.
22. J. Hone, *W.B. Yeats 1865-1939*, 266.
23. George Eliot, *Middle March*, (London: OUP, 1970), 52-53.
24. John Unterecker, *A Reader's Guide to W.B. Yeats*, 129.

5

Easter and After

I

The Easter Rising brought Yeats back again to the common man. In fact, it surprised him, so sudden it was. Not only Yeats but also the large majority of the Irish people did not know what was going underground. What was more surprising was that the working class took the lead this time and those who came from the upper class declassed themselves. While Martin Murphy and Tim Healy and the Unionists were limiting their activities to certain reforms, the other political parties; more patriotic and revolutionary, were planning to liberate Ireland by armed revolution. Prominent among them was the Irish Republican Brotherhood which had rejected John Mitchel's dictum that England's difficulty was Ireland's opportunity on the ground that it would be too late to wait for the proper opportunity. The supreme council of the I.R.B. decided unanimously that only a sacrifice would unite Ireland. The other revolutionary parties, Sinn Fein and Labour, too, felt the same way. They also said that Mitchel's dictum had betrayed the cause of Ireland. After the failure of the Volunteer Movement, there was a split and the more determined minority stayed with Eoin MacNeil. Because of the unanimity in ideology, the I.R.B., the Volunteers and the Labour Citizen Army decided for an armed revolution as soon as war appeared likely.

There were a few hitches in the beginning. Although he had denounced the action of the Parliamentary Party in his paper Sinn Fein, Arthur Griffith did not collaborate with MacNeil. The I.R.B. feared that impetuous James Connolly, leader of Labour Citizen Army, might lead the rebellion too early, and that would be a premature rebellion. The only wayout was to kidnap and hold him till he agreed to co-operate in unison. The I.R.B. did it exactly. The other problem was MacNeil. He wanted to take arms only when full preparation was made and arms and ammunition reached from Germany. But the I.R.B. held a different view. To quote Brian Inglis:

> It was determined to carry through its plans even if they were obviously doomed to failure, on the assumption that a blood sacrifice would attract, or share waverers into the cause of the Republic. Patrick Pearse, in particular, had more than once expressed his conviction that such a sacrifice might be necessary. In his panegyric at the grave of the Fenian, O' Danovan Rossa, in 1915, he said 'Life springs from death; and from the graves of patriot men and women spring living nations,' and on other occasions he had indicated that more graves might have to be dug before the nation could live.[1]

Yeats, who had met Connolly earlier, must have come to know his speech. He almost repeated Connolly's words in "The Rose Tree":

> O plain as plain can be
> There's nothing but our own red blood
> Can make a right Rose Tree. (*C.P.* 206)

Easter 1916 was the date decided for the armed rebellion. It was reported that an arms-loaded ship from Germany was coming to help the rebels. Later, MacNeil was told that the British interpreted the code and arrested Sir Roger Casement. Upon this he countermanded the rebellion. But it was too late. Unheeding MacNeil's orders the army under the leadership of Patrick Pearse, James Connolly, Thomas MacDonagh, Thomas J. Clarke, Sean MacBride and Con Markiewiez marched to the General Post Office, Dublin, on Easter Monday. From its steps Pearse proclaimed the birth of the Irish Republic as a sovereign state.

The revolutionaries held the Post Office out for about a week. The rising was soon crushed and the authorities retaliated it by executing Pearse, Connolly, Clarke, MacBride, MacDonagh and other revolutionaries, not at a time, but in one or two in cold blood. This action of the British government infuriated the entire nation and a strong wave of sympathy swept all over. These martyrs became new heroes in the line of Emmet, Fitzgerald and Tone. Yeats wrote to Lady Gregory on 11 May 1916. The letter is quoted in full:

> My dear Lady Gregory,
>
> The Dublin tragedy has been a great sorrow and anxiety. Cosgrave, whom I saw a few months ago in connection with the Municipal Gallery project and found our best supporter, has got many years' imprisonment and today I see that an old friend Dixon—unless there are two of the name—who began with me the whole work of the literary movement has been shot in a barrack yard without trial of any kind. I have little doubt there have been many miscarriages of justice. The wife of a Belgian Minister of war told me a few days ago that three British officers had told her that the command of the British army in France should be made over the French generals and that French generals have told her that they await with great anxiety the result of the coming German attack on the English lines because of the incompetence of the English Higher Command as a whole. Haig however they believed in—he was recommended by the French for the post. I see therefore no reason to believe that the delicate instrument of Justice is being worked with precision in Dublin. I am trying to write a poem on the men executed—"terrible beauty has been born again." If the English conservative party had made a declaration that they did not intend to rescind the Home Rule Bill there would have been no Rebellion. I had no idea that any public event could so deeply move me—and I am very despondent about the future. At the moment I feel that all the work of years has been overturned, all the bringing together of classes, all the freeing of Irish literature and criticism from politics. Maud Gonne reminds me that she saw the revived houses about O'Connell Street and the wounded and the dying lying about the streets, in the first few days of the war.... Her main thought seems to be 'tragic dignity has returned to Ireland.'[2]

Yeats personally knew many of the leaders who were executed in the abortive rising. He writes about Pearse and Connolly:

> Three or four years after the betrayal of Parnell two little boys, sons of a Dublin stone mason, knelt down beside their beds and prayed that they might sacrifice their lives for Ireland. In their early twenties I saw them occasionally; they would come to the Abbey Theatre for some reason or other. I think they hired it for some reason or other. The elder had founded a school for boys where Irish heroic tales were taught, Cuchulain remained an example to be followed, and was also a poet, sometimes in Gaelic, sometimes in English.... Just one year when I was passing through Dublin on my way to London from Galway, where I spent my summers, someone said, 'There's going to be troubles—Pearse is going through Ireland, preaching the blood sacrifice—he says blood must be shed in every generation.' Some [time] after that came the 1916 rebellion. Several actors belonging to my theatre had part; one of the best was killed.... Pearse wrote the night before his killing those strange verses ignoring death....[3]

The Easter poems, according to Graham Hough, "give the lie to some of his earlier convictions about political poetry" and that "he attempts the exaltation not of individuals, but of a people." I find it difficult to agree with this view of his. In fact, these poems reiterate Yeats's idea, formed in the eighteen eightees, that only men of heroic mould can revive the old glory of Ireland. We see the comic figures transformed into heroes in "Easter 1916." Yeats began writing it on 11 May and finally completed it on 25 September, 1916. The long time taken in writing and reaching the final version indicates that Yeats did not want to publish it for immediate popularity; on the other hand he put in all his energy to make it a piece of art that would be of permanent value. The title "Easter 1916" and the date 25 September are significant. Roland Barthes, while analysing Poe's "Valdemar," propounds the idea that a proper name is the prince of signifiers and key to the main theme of a text. Here the title "Easter 1916" and its publication in September remind us of "September 1913" where Yeats lamented the decline of heroism and the rise of opportunism. Here the contrast between the attitudes of 1913 and 1916 is obvious. The first stanza is a revealing self-commentary:

> I have met them at close of day
> Coming with vivid faces
> From counter or desk among grey
> Eighteenth century houses.
> I have passed with a nod of the head
> Or polite meaningless words
> Or have lingered a while and said
> Polite meaningless words. (*C.P.* 202-03)

The word "them" shows the distance between the poet and the martyrs. This distance is further emphasised in the last four lines by the nodding of head and polite meaningless words; we come to know that there was no intimate relationship between them and the poet and there existed a kind of familiarity only. In the subsequent six lines they are considered comic figures, inhabitants of the land where "motley is worn." But their heroic deed strikes the poet with awe. The transformation is so sudden and grand that he cannot but marvel at the scene:

> All changed, changed utterly
> A terrible beauty is born.

These lines which function as refrain in the poem are in sharp contrast with the refrain "Romantic Ireland's dead and gone/ It's with O'Leary in the grave" in September 1913. Easter is the day of Christ's resurrection and here is the resurrection of the heroic Ireland. When we read the stanza second time, we find that the change is not only in situation and the comic figures but in the poet too. The people whom he considered to be comic figures are now heroes of tragic dignity. In the next section the remoteness is shortened. The martyrs who were referred to as "they" and "them", a group of insignificant people, become familiar with their individual traits in the second section. The use of the personal pronoun is significant. He remembers the young days of "the woman" (Con Markiewicz) when she had a sweet voice and was a treat to watch when she rode a horse and, also, her later days, when she took active part in trade unionism. He considered that it was unworthy of her to mix with the crowd and maintained that it was her "ignorant goodwill" that led her to take part in trade union activities*. In the same way he praises the school teacher Pearse, a poet, and his compatriot Connolly for their noble action:

> This man had kept a school
> And rode our winged horse
> This other his helper and friend
> Was coming into his force. (*C.P.* 203)

He is full of admiration even for MacBride whom Maud Gonne married and who, for him, was a "rainglorious lout":

> He too has resigned his part
> In the carnal comedy;
> He too has been changed in his turn
> Transformed utterly: (*C.P.* 203)

The third stanza, which is without refrain, describes the poet's ideal and the martyr's achievement. These martyrs, all men of action, remain unchanged in the pursuit of the ideal amidst the world of change:

> Hearts with one purpose alone
> Through summer and winter seem
> Enchanted to a stone
> To trouble the living stream. (*C.P.* 204)

Life is a stream that flows on gently but sometimes it is troubled if a big stone comes in its way. The stone changes its course. These martyrs fixed to the "enchanted stone" have created history. The image of the stone is further enlarged and made richer in meaning in the subsequent lines of the stanza. The stone symbolises the heroic ideals which remain constant and which regularly trouble the common course of life which changes regularly.

The concluding stanza is the synthesis of conflicting emotions and ideas. At first, the poet doubts the use and validity of such a sacrifice:

---

* Yeats was certainly wrong in his estimate of Con Markiewicz. She, being a revolutionary, declassed herself and worked for the uplift of the downtrodden. She became a cabinet minister for her services to Ireland.

Too long a sacrifice
Can make a stone of heart
O when may it suffice?

But the answer comes soon that the Irish people should do their duty first:

That is heaven's part, our part
To murmur name upon name,
As a mother names her child
When sleep at last has come
On limbs that had run wild. (*C.P.* 204)

The image of a mother repeating her child's name after sleep shows the tenderness of feeling after the final sleep of the Easter martyrs.

Then the question, "Was it needless death after all?" is a comment on his own reluctance to bloodshed and violence. Earlier he had differed with Maud Gonne and advised her to abstain from subversive activities but, now, the heroic act of the revolutionaries has changed his mind:

We know their dream; enough
To know they dreamed and are dead
And what if excess of love
Bewildered them till they died? (*C.P.* 204)

The concluding stanza brings us closer to the figures in the first stanza; the distance between them and the poet is reduced and what is a national loss becomes a personal loss too. They are named with tender love and affection:

I write it out in a verse—
MacDonagh and MacBride
And Connolly and Pearse
Now and in time to be,
Wherever green is worn
Are changed, changed utterly
A terrible beauty is born. (*C.P.* 205)

The poem is so structured as to lead us step by step from the comic to the tragic, from the distant to the close and from the indifferent to the intimate. The distant comic characters to whom Yeats had indifferent attitude are all transformed into great heroes. In the first stanza there are two kinds of actants with different functions. The first are the comic figures and the second is the observer, the poet himself. He is amused to see them coming from the eighteenth century house. They belong to the country where motley is worn. But suddenly they change into heroic figures. The change is so sudden and unexpected that the poet is wonder-struck. In the subsequent stanza; the transformed characters act in full glory. The poet, a passive observer, does not remain indifferent. There is a great change in him too. The reader begins to take more interest in the cognitive function of the poet. It is the conflicting emotions and ideas and their synthesis at the end that gives a coherence to the structure of the poem.

"Sixteen Dead Men" completed on 17 December, 1917 is another poem written on the death of the revolutionaries. Although not a great poem like "Easter 1916," it is charged with patriotic feelings and shows Yeats's active involvement in Irish politics. It is an impassioned speech to arouse patriotism in the Irish people:

O but we talked at large before
The sixteen men were shot,
But who can talk of give and take,
What should be and what not
While those dead men are loitering there
To stir the boiling pot. (*C.P.* 205)

The Unionists' argument that the Irish people should remain silent till the end of the First World War is rejected in the second stanza. There is no time nor need to wait for the end of the war:

You say that we should still the land
Till Germany's overcome;
But who is there to argue that
Now Pearse is deaf and dumb?
And is their logic to outweigh
MacDonagh's bony thumb? (*C.P.* 205)

By placing the martyrs in the rank of Fitzgerald and Tone he indirectly exhorts the Irish people to support the cause of Ireland and if they do so, they too will be counted with the heroes of the past:

How could you dream they'd listen
That have an ear alone
For those new comrades they have found,
Lord Edward and Wolfe Tone
Or meddle with our give and take
That converse bone to bone? (*C.P.* 205)

What is remarkable in this poem is its incantory quality. Written in iambic tetrameters and trimeters lines which occur alternately the poem moves elegiacally. The use of monosyllabic words gives it a simple dignity. Secondly, the even lines are made to rhyme with the aim to close an idea that begins in the odd lines. If the poem were written in the heroic couplet or even in blank verse, the movement would be slow, heavy and lachrymous. Here, Yeats's intention is, besides mourning the tragedy of the patriots, to arouse patriotic feelings and lead his country people to action, and he is successful in doing so by making innovation in the metrical pattern.

"The Rose Tree" (7 April, 1917) is a dialogue between Pearse and Connolly. Yeats shares the view of Pearse and Connolly that the rebellion may be unsuccessful but it will lead ultimately to the liberation of Ireland. In the first stanza Pearse speaks of the troubles in Ireland, which are created by narrow-minded politicians (perhaps, the Murphy group) who lack heroic ideals. The other cause of the troubles is the British government, "a wind that blows across the sea." Connolly's reply, apparently simple and innocent, is significant and its full meaning is realized in the concluding stanza. His suggestion that the rose tree needs watering is understood when he replies to Pearse's question, "But where can we draw water/When all the wells are parched away?" We realise immediately that he is talking of blood sacrifice for the rejuvenation of Ireland:

O plain as plain can be
There's nothing but our own red blood
Can make a right Rose Tree. (*C.P.* 206)

In the early poems the rose is something mysterious, incomprehensible and intangible and we have to read Yeats's rosicrucian explication to understand its symbolical meaning but here it is plain and clear. Although a part of Yeats's esotericism, it has an independent existence in this poem and the main reason for it is that Yeats has assimilated all his political experiences in its composition which he was unable to do in his young days. Retaining the tenderness of humanity (the second stanza is a beautiful picture of rose tree in a garden), he praises the blood sacrifice of Pearse and Connolly. What adds beauty to the poem is its form, a dialogue between two patriots. The poet does not say anything from his own side; he is only an audience.

The Easter poems outlive their time. No doubt, they deal with a major theme, sacrifice of the Irish heroes, but what is more important is the artistic presentation of the sacrifice of the martyrs and Yeats's sincerity of feeling. The heroes whom he admires had not impressed him much and for MacBride he had ill-feeling as he had married Maud Gonne. It is their selfless sacrifice and heroic act that raised them high in his eyes. He, later, in a more complex poem "The Statues" made his viewpoint more clear:

When Pearse summoned Cuchulain to his side,
What stalked through the Post Office? What intellect
What calculation, number, measurement replied?
We Irish, born into that ancient sect
But thrown upon this filthy modern tide
And by its formless spawning fury wrecked,
Climb to our proper dark, that we may trace
The lineaments of a plummet-measured face.

(*C.P.* 375-76)

Here, Yeats associates Pearse with the people of heroic mould who seek for the unity of being—"a plummet-measured face."*

The two other poems "On a Political Prisoner" and "The Leader of the Crowd" expose the limitations of Yeats's political ideas and women's role in active politics. The political prisoner Constance Markiewicz whom he met in her youth, is criticised for mixing with the crowd. Constance and her sister Eva both inherited their father's love of the poor and the down-trodden. After her marriage Constance became Countess Markiewicz and lived with her husband Count Casimir Markiewicz in Russia for

* The poem is analysed in detail in Chapter 8.

sometime. Later on, both moved to Dublin where they engaged themselves in social and literary activities. Different kinds of people—writers, painters, politicians and trade unionists—gathered at their place and discussed the important issues of the time. Eva Gore-Booth also followed her sister's path. Both sisters devoted time to social and political activities; they organized the Irish Scout Movement and regularly visited the slum areas of Dublin to help the dwellers. Esther Roper writes about Con Markiewicz:

> From 1913 she had identified herself with the Trade Union Movement, whose leader was James Connolly. For six months (at the time of the great strike there) she had almost single-handed run a canteen for the feeding of the starving children—collecting the money, buying and cooking the food herself.... She was an honorary official of the Transport Worker's Union and an officer in their Citizen Army. (Later she was in the first Republican Cabinet as Minister for Labour and did very able work.)[4]

Because her ideas were radically different from those of Yeats, she did not join the Abbey, but wrote rebel propagandist plays such as *Blood Money, The Invisible Mother* and *Broken Dreams.*[5] Yeats expected her to join his group and remain an aristocrat. But she declassed herself and adopted the working class ways. In the Easter Rising she was made Second in Command of the Citizen Army Force. After the defeat she was courtmartialled and sentenced to death. The sixteen rebels were executed but the rest, notable among them Eamon De Valera, William Cosgrave and Con Markiewicz, were sent to jail after a review of their case.

"On a Political Prisoner" shows Yeats's ambivalent attitude. He remembers her when she was young, majestic and passionate at the same time:

> When long ago I saw her ride
> Under Ben Bulben to the meet,
> The beauty of her country-side
> With all youth's lonely wilderness stirred,
> She seemed to have grown clean and sweet
> Like any rock-bred, sea-borne bird. (*C.P.* 207)

She was like a brave fearless gull which mapped the sea and the sky in a solo flight and it was a treat to watch her riding a horse in those days:

> Sea-borne, or balanced on the air
> When first it sprang out of the nest
> Upon some lofty rock to stare
> Upon the cloudy canopy,
> While under its storm-beaten breast
> Cried out the hollows of the sea. (*C.P.* 207)

But at present she is a different woman. Now she is a grey gull (the pun is obvious), sitting in a cell and nibbling the food given to her. The contrast is sad indeed. Once a free and spirited aristocrat riding majestically in her estate, she is now counting her days in prison. In the poet's opinion she has declined in her ideas too. Now she is:

> ...a bitter, and abstract thing
> Her thought a popular enmity
> Blind and leader of the blind
> Drinking the foul ditch where they lie. (*C.P.* 207)

Although the poem is technically superb, it fails to assess the qualities of the great lady. By criticising her Yeats has damaged himself. A poet must be objective in writing about others. It is really surprising that he glorified "that vainglorious lout MacBride" in "Easter 1916" but denounced Con Markiewicz in "On a Political Prisoner." The second poem "The Leaders Of The Crowd" further exposes the hollowness of Yeats's penchant for aristocracy. His disapproval of the common people's ideas and activities is not convincing. Even this beautiful image:

> How can they know
> Truth flourishes where the student's lamp has shone
> And there alone, that have no solitude? (*C.P.* 207-08)

fails to show that Con Markiewicz's ideas were abstract and bitter or that she led the Irish people to a wrong path.

Yeats realised his mistake later on. In 1927 he wrote the poem "In Memory of Eva Gore-Booth and Con Markiewicz" to correct his mistake. Eva Gore-Booth, Constance's younger sister, was a poet and like her sister took part in active politics. She worked for Women's Suffrage Movement and the struggling trade unions since 1899 and visited Constance regularly when she was in jail after Easter Rising. Eva's death in 1926 and of Constance in 1927 moved Yeats greatly. He remembered the days he had spent in their house. Earlier he had written to Eva:

> Your sister and yourself, two beautiful figures among the great trees of Lissadell, are among the dear memories of my youth.

The opening lines depict his sense impressions:

> The light of evening, Lissadell
> Great windows open to the south
> Two girls in silk kimonos, both
> Beautiful, one a gazelle. (*C.P.* 263)

The lines which follow the quoted passage express the poet's sadness at the loss of the past glory:

> But a raving autumn shears
> Blossom from the summer's wealth (*C.P.* 263)

He is really grieved at the sad fate of Constance:

> The older is condemned to death,
> Pardoned, drags out lonely years
> Conspiring among the ignorant. (*C.P.* 263)

Here the tone is not of anger nor of scorn but of distress that the talented nobility who should have devoted her life to aristocratic virtues has fallen among the ignorant people and her thought and action are not worthy of her. He has the same feeling for Eva:

> I know not what the younger dreams—
> Some vague Utopia—and she seems,
> When withered old and skeleton gaunt,
> An image of such policies. (*C.P.* 263)

Here, too, Yeats is critical of Eva's ideology. He calls her project "some vague Utopia." If we follow Derrida, we can say that Yeats does not fully comprehend Eva's dreams and, finding no better words, calls them "vague Utopia." We all know that all great people have their Utopia, though it may be vague. The tone changes after this:

> Dear shadows, now you know it all,
> All the folly of a fight

With a common wrong or right
The innocent and the beautiful
Have no enemy but time. (*C.P.* 264)

Now, there is a reconciliation with the "dear shadows" of Constance and Eva when time has passed and he has attained maturity. He realises the fact that they all (including Yeats) strove for the revival of the heroic Ireland:

Arise and bid me strike a match
And strike another till time catch;
Should the conflagration climb
Run till all the sages know.
We the great gazebo built
They convicted us of guilt
Bid me strike a match and blow. (*C.P.* 264)

It will be relevant here to quote Jon Stallworthy's comment on this passage, which supports my interpretation that Yeats, after his experience of the civil war, revised his opinion about the Gore-Booth sisters:

> In the midst of his tragic reflections Yeats finds his imagination caught in a heroic and apocalyptic vision. The two girls shall be revenged on their enemy. Saul suggests that "We the great gazebo built" means "We provided the lofty outlook;" and one level I believe Yeats means the gazebo to represent his early vision, more romantic than realistic, of a resurgent Ireland. From the detachment of their ivory tower, he and such of his friends as the Gore-Booth sisters, had imagined their countrymen casting off the yoke of England, fired by the spirits of Cuchulain and the ancient heroes.[6]

II

Although Yeats felt the effect of the First World War, he did not write a single poem on it. The reason was that he was more concerned with Ireland's freedom and her cultural identity. He said in one of his interviews:

> I hate international literature. The core of a thing must be national or local. But at the same time it ought to be a fundamental piece of human life, which is the same everywhere.[7]

He paid little attention to the First World War because it did not affect Ireland as an independent country and if a few Irishmen fought for England it was not for the love of the British empire. Yeats's attitude to the war was that of indifference:

> Those that I fight I do not hate,
> Those that I guard I do not love
> My country is Kiltartan Cross
> My countrymen Kiltartan's poor. (*C.P.* 152)

His poetry written during the First World War and after can be best understood in the context of the contemporary Irish political situation. For him the Easter Rising was more important than the war between England and Germany.

The events that followed the Easter Rising and the world war worsened the political situation of Ireland. The Irish public opinion was ignited to a big fire; the leaders resorted to violent means to free their nation. Apart from his active involvement in the Irish national movement, Yeats was working with his system which he summarised in *A Vision.* This system is a combination of myth, history and esotericism and interprets the progress of history in the form of a cycle. He seriously believed that the old civilization had reached its end and that the new era would by no means be a better one. He expressed his apprehension in a letter to George Russell:

> What I want is that Ireland be kept from giving itself (under the influence of its lunatic faculty of going against everything it believes England to affirm) to Marxian revolution or Marxian definitions of value as in this age the spearhead of materialism and leading to inevitable murder.[8]

The first draft of "The Second Coming" refers to Lenin's surrender to the Germans:

> The germans are ( ) now to Russia come
> Though everybody some innocent has died
> ( ) and murder.[9]

After October Revolution, Lenin surrendered Finland, Esthonia, Courtland, Lithuania and tracts of Russian Poland to the Germans on 3 March, 1918. Yeats feared that this surrender would lead to the further downfall of the Russian aristocracy. He felt that the world war, the worsening Irish situation and growing materialism had completely changed the world scenario and the old things he valued most were going to perish. This fear is there in "A Prayer For My Daughter." But the vision in the concluding lines of "The Second Coming" is really ill-boding:

...but now I know
That twenty centuries of stony sleep
Were vexed to nightmare by a rocking cradle
And what rough beast, its hour come round at last,
Slouches towards Bethlehem to be born?" (*C.P.* 210)

To come to the political situation of Ireland, the nation was on the top of the volcano of violence in 1919. Though the top leaders of the Easter Rising were executed by the British government, the Sinn Fein Party gathered a greater strength under the leadership of Eamon de Valera; it won seventy-three seats in the election but refused to attend the Parliament or to recognize in any way the authority of the British Parliament. In the meantime another problem arose. The Unionists of Ulster and the Sinn Feiners of the South quarrelled over certain political issues. Lloyd George, Britain's Prime Minister, tried to solve the problem by setting up two Parliaments, one for the six Protestants countries of the North-Eastern Ireland, the other for the rest of Ireland. There were provisions for common action and ultimate combination. Northern Ireland set up its Parliament under the act, but the Sinn Fein party refused to have anything to do with the scheme, broke into open rebellion, declared Ireland independent and elected a President of the Irish republic and a representative body called Dail Eirann. Without considering the consequences, Lloyd George poured troops in Ireland, and when most of the Irish people resigned, he raised an auxiliary force (called Black and Tans as they wore black berets and Khaki uniforms) that consisted of the demobilised army officers. The Black and Tans launched a campaign of systematic reprisals which culminated in setting fire to the city of Cork. The poem "Reprisals," though written on the death of Robert Gregory, describes the brutalities of the Black and Tans:

Half-drunk or whole mad soldiery
Are murdering your tenants there;

Where many new-married women sit
And suckle children now? Armed men
May murder them in passing by
Nor law nor parliament take heed.

(Variorum Edition, 791)

The situation distressed Yeats greatly and he felt that his dream of a heroic Ireland would not come true. He wrote to Olivia Shakespeare on 9 April, 1921:

> I am writing a series of poems (Thought suggested by the Present State of the World or some such name). I have written two and there may be many more. They are not philosophical but simple and passionate, a lamentation over lost peace and lost hope.[10]

The poem referred to in the letter was published in the *Dial* under the title "Nineteen Hundred and Nineteen." The poem is so titled to show that anarchy in Ireland began in 1919 and in this respect is closely linked to "The Second Coming." "Nineteen Hundred and Nineteen" may be divided structurally into three parts, although it consists of six sections. The first part describes the sorrow for the decline of culture, the second the brutality of the Black and Tans and misdeeds of the Irish volunteers, and the third a vision of evil. The first stanza of section I laments the loss of the beautiful works of the ancient Greek artists, the works that stood the test of time:

Many ingenious lovely things are gone
That seemed sheer miracle to the multitude,
Protected from the circle of the moon
That pitches common things about. (*C.P.* 232-33)

The last two lines of the stanza refer to Phidias and his art:

And gone are Phidias' famous ivories
And all the golden grasshoppers and bees.

Juxtaposed with Greece is the eighteenth century Ireland in the second stanza—"We too had too many pretty toys when young." But the matter does not end here; there is the loss of culture and habit of good thought:

A law indifferent to blame or praise,
To bribe or threat; habits that made old wrong

Melt down, as it were wax in the sun's rays;
Public opinion ripening for so long
We thought it would outlive all future days. (*C.P.* 233)

Those good old days are gone:

Now days are dragon-ridden, the nightmare
Rides upon sleep: a drunken soldiery
Can leave the mother, murdered at her door,
To crawl in her own blood, and go scot-free. (*C.P.* 233)

The Irish men of letters had hoped to unite Ireland culturally but now they find that the whole country has gone wild and violent like weasels fighting in a hole. The theme of disintegration further develops in the fifth stanza:

...; who knows no work can stand
Whether health, wealth or peace of mind were spent
On master-work of intellect or hand,
No honour leave its mighty monument
Has but one comfort left; all triumph would
But break upon his ghostly solitude. (*C.P.* 234)

In the next stanza, even the comfort that "all triumph would/ But break upon his ghostly solitude" is doubted, and the attitude is of resignation:

But is there any comfort to be found?
Man is in love and loves what vanishes
What more is there to say? (*C.P.* 234)

The idea of the dying heroic age continues in the second section. Lois Fuller's Chinese dancers are whirled around by "a dragon of air" which has "hurried them off on its own furious path." He is reminded of the Platonic year and says:

So the Platonic year
Whirls out new right and wrong,
Whirls in the old instead. (*C.P.* 234)

All men, he feels are helpless dancers in the circle of history. To prove this he links the dragon of Lois Fuller's painting to the dragon-ridden days of the first section and conveys the idea that Irish people, like the Chinese dancers, have created "a dragon of air" that has fallen among them and hurried them round to its own furious path.

In the third section, the swan, the symbol of the soul, could have made Yeats hopeful if its breast were "thrust out in pride" in defiance of the present crisis. But it is not so; the swan "has leaped into the desolate heaven." The present state of Ireland has worsened so much that it seems that it is beyond correction:

> O but we dreamed to mend
> Whatever mischief seemed
> To afflict mankind, but now
> That winds of winter blow
> Learn that we were crack-pated when we dreamed.
> (*C.P.* 235)

The fourth section by reference to the "weasek's twist, the weasel's tooth" is closely connected with the first section and the repetition of the weasel image affirms the domination of the animal side of man. Therefore, Yeats invites all the people to mock at the great, the wise, the good and, finally, at the mockers themselves as all the values of life are at stake and they have nothing positive before them:

> Mock mockers after that
> That would not lift a hand may be
> To help good, wise or great
> To bar that foul storm out, for we
> Traffic in mockery. (*C.P.* 236)

The poem ends with the vision of evil. The images of violence accumulate and whirl together to dissolve in chaos and out of that chaos are born, not the Sun, the Moon and the Stars, but images that beget worse images. At first come the handsome riders who run round and round in their course to vanish; then come Herodias' daughters with a sudden blast of dusty wind and by the time the dust settles there appears Evil*:

> But now wind drops, dust settles; thereupon
> There lurches past, his great eyes without thought

* Yeats writes in the "Notes": "The country people see at times certain apparitions whom they name now "fallen angels," now "ancient inhabitants of the country," and describe as riding at whiles "with flowers upon the heads of horses." I have assumed in the sixth poem that these horsemen now that the times worsen, give way to worse. My last symbol, Robert Artisson, was an evil much run after in Kilkenny at start of the fourteenth century." (*C.P.* 534-35)

> Under the shadow of stupid straw-pale locks,
> That insolent friend Robert Artisson
> To whom the love-lorn Lady Kyteler brought
> Bronzed peacock feathers, red combs of her cocks.
>
> (*C.P.* 237)

Professor A.G. Stock remarks that "taken as a continuous meditation the six parts all but lose coherence."[11] But with all my regard to her scholarship, I find it difficult to agree with her. It is the imagery of the poem that gives it organicity. The first section is the statement of the loss of the Irish heroic tradition and culture. The second section continues the theme of the decline of culture. The third section is a search for unity in the chaotic world. The fourth section comes back again to the Irish scene where people have degenerated so low that what was a matter of shame for them in past, has become a source of pleasure; they "shriek with pleasure" if they show "the weasel's twist, the weasel's tooth." Men who once appreciated the beautiful works of art have degraded themselves by trafficking in mockery. The sixth section recapitulates the previous sections with the image of "violence upon the roads" and reaches its end with the vision of Artisson. The difference between the visions of the "rough beast" of "The Second Coming" and Robert Artisson in "Nineteen Hundred and Nineteen" is that the people wince and become indignant in the first poem but they are attracted towards evil in the latter.

The war against the British rule continued till 1921. The British Prime Minister intervened and persuaded the Sinn Fein leaders to negotiate with him. Arthur Griffith led the delegation, but Eamon de Valera refused to be one of the party and privately directed the members not to sign any document without the approval of the Dublin cabinet. Arthur Griffith and Michael Collins had to come many times to Dublin for consultation. Yeats watched the activities with grave concern. He wrote to Olivia Shakespeare:

> I am in deep gloom about Ireland, for though I expect ratification of the treaty from a plebiscite, I see no hope of escape from bitterness, and the extreme party may carry the country. When men are very bitter, death and ruin

> draw them on as a rabbit is supposed to be drawn on by the dancing of the fox.*

The treaty was signed in desperation by Griffith and Collins. It was agreed that Ireland would have dominion status but Ulster would be excluded. The cabinet of Dublin split over the decision. De Valera's group opposed Griffith and Collins on the ground that Ulster was separated. Besides this, the most objectionable part of the treaty was the Oath of Allegiance to the King,** which everyone opposed. The enmity between the Pro-Treaty Group and the Anti-Treaty Group grew violent. To avoid a Civil War a pact was made between De Valera and Collins that the parties should not oppose in the constituencies but before the pact could come into force, the Civil War broke out. Arthur Griffith died suddenly on 12 August, 1922 and ten days later Michael Collins was shot dead. In retaliation the National Army persecuted many Anti-Treaty leaders. The bad situation distressed Yeats. What he had foreseen in his letter to Olivia Shakespeare appeared in its ugliness in the form of the Civil War. He wrote to her on 9 October, 1922:

> "My dear Olivia,
>
> I spent the summer correcting proofs and writing a series of poems called "Meditations in Time of Civil War" which I shall send to the *Mercury*. Now I am busy writing out the system....
>
> The situation here is very curious...a revolt against democracy by a small section. Under the direction of an Erskine Childers they burn houses that they may force the majority to say, 'It is too expensive to remain Free State, let us turn republican.' At any rate that is believed to be the policy. I have met some of the ministers who more and more seem too sober to meet the wildness of these enemies;

* Quoted. J. Hone, *W.B. Yeats,* 340.

** The Oath ran as follows: " I will be faithful to His Majesty King George V, his heirs and successors by law, in virtue of the common citizenship of Ireland with Great Britain and her adherence to and membership of the group of nations forming the British Commonwealth of Nations." Quoted by Terence de Vere White, *Ireland,* 81.

> and everywhere one notices a drift towards conservatism, perhaps towards Autocracy. I always knew that it would come, but not that it would come in this tragic way. One wonders what prominent man will live through it. One meets a minister at dinner, passing his armed guard on the doorstep, and one feels no certainty that one will meet him again. We are entering on the final and most dreadful stage. Perhaps there is nothing so dangerous to a modern state, when politics take the place of theology, as a bunch of martyrs. A bunch of martyrs (1916) were the bomb and we are living in the explosion....
>
> Yours
>
> W.B. Yeats[12]

As the letter shows "Meditations In Time of Civil War" is a meditation on the contemporary political events of national importance. Yeats views the entire situation from a philosophical point of view. But he is careful enough not to make philosophy ride over the stream of emotions.

Divided into seven sections, each with a title, the poem presents the different moods of Yeats.

The first section, titled "Ancestral Houses"; takes up, to quote A.G. Stock, the same theme of the ruined ancestral houses but this time the ruin is no longer an impending horror, but an accomplished fact."[13] The ancestral houses are the symbol of the rich Irish tradition. They were constructed by cultured men of aristocracy and became centres of artistic creation:

Some violent bitter man, some powerful man
Called architect and artist, in that they,
Bitter and violent men, might rear in stone
The sweetness that longed for night and day,
The gentleness none there had ever known. (*C.P.* 225)

Now those aristocratic men are no more and their inheritors have adopted a different path:

But when the master's buried mice can play,
And may be the great-grandson of that house,
For all its bronze and marble, 's but a mouse. (*C.P.* 236)

The repetition of the word "what" stresses the bitterness in the poet's heart. The underlying irony in the last two stanzas moves us deeply. All the old beautiful works of art that are pride of a nation have no value for the present generation of Ireland:

O what if levelled lawns and gravelled ways
Where slippered Contemplation finds his ease
And Childhood a delight for every sense,
But take our greatness with our violence? (*C.P.* 226)

And the final stanza ends,

What if those things the greatest of mankind
Consider most to magnify, or to bless,
But take our greatness with our bitterness? (*C.P.* 226)

He comes from the general to the personal because he, too, is a carrier of the tradition. Sections II, III and IV depict his apprehension of the future. First, he describes his house, a tower with a chamber at the top reached by a winding stair, is the place where "the symbolic rose can break in flower." We know that the tower is the symbol of tradition, the chamber is the place of artistic creation, the winding stair of argument and the rose a symbol of life. The third section, "My Table," is a meditation on art and life. Using Sato's sword as the symbol of art, he posits the idea that poetry is created by an anguished heart:

Chaucer had not drawn breath
When it was forged. In Sato's house,
Curved like new moon, moon-luminous,
It lay five hundred years.
Yet if no change appears
No moon; only an aching heart
Conceives a changeless work of art. (*C.P.* 228)

The fourth section titled "My Descendant" anticipates "Lapis Lazuli." There is the fear that his descendants may not carry on the tradition which he has inherited and nourished:

And what if my descendants lose the flower
Through natural declension of the soul,
Through too much business with the passing hour,
Through too much play, or marriage with a fool?
May this laborious stair and this stark tower

Become a roofless ruin that the owl
May build in the cracked masonry and cry
Her desolation to the desolate sky. (*C.P.* 229)

In this troubled fear his solace is love of his wife, Georgie Hyde Lees, friend Lady Gregory and the tower that symbolises Irish tradition and his own poetry that will survive:

And I that count myself most prosperous,
Seeing that love and friendship are enough,
For an old neighbour's friendship chose the house
And decked and altered it for a girl's love,
And know whatever flourish and decline
These stones remain their monument and mine.
(*C.P.* 229)

In the next section he shifts his attention to the road by his house. As a senator he is given protection by the government. But he finds fault with both the Republicans and the National Army because both are destroying the cause of Ireland. He comments on a fat soldier rather wrvly:

An affable irregular,
A heavily-built Falstaffian man,
Comes cracking jokes of civil war
As though to die by gunshot were
The finest play under the sun. (*C.P.* 229)

A lieutenant of the National Army and his soldiers come to him and ask if he has any trouble. He replies in such a way that we may be misled and will think that he is evading the issue. But the reply, a fine example of understatement, is highly symbolical:

I complain
Of the foul weather, hail and rain
A pear-tree broken by the storm. (*C.P.* 230)

The "foul weather" and "the storm" symbolise the civil war, "hail and rain" fighting factions and the "pear-tree" humanity. He turns back to his chamber "caught/In the cold snows of a dream."

The sixth section is a prayer for sweetness and light. The bees in the Seven Woods had given him consolation. He invokes them again to bring sweetness and harmony in life:

We had fed the heart on fantasies,
The heart's grown brutal from the fare,
More substance in our enemities
Than in our love: O honey-bees
Come build in the empty house of the store (*C.P.* 230-31)

The seventh section moves almost like the later part of section V of *The Waste Land.* But, I must hasten to say, that the similarity is only in the experienced feelings of the protagonists. The protagonist of *The Waste Land* sits silently and watches the fall of the western civilization. Yeats, too, sees the collapse of the western civilization, symbolised by the nightmarish condition prevailing in Ireland. He sees in a vision:

The cloud-pale unicorns; the eyes of acquamarine,
The quivering half-closed eyelids, the rags of cloud
or of lace,
Or eyes that rage has brightened, arms it has made lean,
Give place to an indifferent multitude, give place
To brazen hawks. Nor self-delighting reverie,
Nor hate of what's to come, nor pity for what's gone,
Nothing but grip of claw, and the eyes of complacency,
The innumerable clanging wings that have put out
the moon. (*C.P.* 232)

But he does not accept defeat. He knows that history moves in a cyclical way. The things that are destroyed today shall be built tomorrow:

The abstract joy
The half-read wisdom of daemonic images
Suffice the ageing man as once growing boy. (*C.P.* 232)

The poems written after Easter 1916 bear testimony to Yeats's active involvement in politics. Active participation in politics made Yeats firmly rooted in ground. But a great thinker and poet he was, he interpreted all the political events philosophically and in the light of Arnold Toynbee's interpretation of history. This is why his political poems transcend their time and assume universality. "Easter 1916," "Nineteen Hundred and Nineteen," "The Second Coming" and "Meditations in Time Of Civil War" have, no doubt their source in contemporary Irish politics, but they are more philosophical in nature. The problem Yeats faces is not a conflict between two groups but the crisis of values, survival of art and culture and degradation of man into beast. Of course, Yeats preferred to focus his attention on the Irish issues. He did so because he was a nationalist and knew his country better. However he was not indifferent to world politics. The first draft of "The Second Coming" refers to Russia's surrender to Germany. Similarly he was keenly interested in Indian politics. It is this involvement in national politics and awareness of the world political situation that gave substance to his poetry and shaped his vision of life. His greatness lies in the fact that he defended human values in the political turmoil of his time. The poems written after 1921 are influenced by current politics but are more philosophical in nature and defend culture and art when everything is at stake.

REFERENCES

1. Brian Inglis, *The Story of Ireland.*
2. A. Wade, ed., *The Letters of W.B. Yeats*, 612-13.
3. R. Skelton, ed., *Modern Ireland: An Address to American Audiences*, 22-23.
4. Esther Roper, *Introduction to Prison Letters of Con Markiewicz*, 4. Quoted by J. Stallworthy, *Between the Lines*, 167.
5. *Ibid.*, 167.
6. *Ibid.*, 167.
7. E. Mikhail, ed., *W.B. Yeats: Interviews and Recollections*, 202.
8. A. Wade, ed., *The Letters of W.B. Yeats*, 152.
9. J. Stallworthy, *Between the Lines*, 17.
10. A. Wade, ed., *The Letters of W.B. Yeats*, 668.
11. A.G. Stock, *W.B. Yeats: His Poetry and Thought*, 182.
12. A. Wade, ed., *The Letters of W.B. Yeats* 689-90.
13. A.G. Stock, *W.B. Yeats: His Poetry and Thought*, 186.

6

Senate and Tower

I

Yeats was nominated a senator of the Irish Free State by the efforts of his friend Oliver Gogarty. His nomination was made on the ground that he had been a member of the Irish Republican Brotherhood, one of the main forces behind the Treaty. Yeats was rather unhappy that his services as poet and leader of the Irish Dramatic Movement were not given due recognition by the government. However, he liked the position. In a letter dated 18 December, 1922, he wrote to Olivia Shakespeare:

> My work on the Senate interests me, a new technique which I am learning in silence—I have only spoken once and then but six sentences and I shall not speak again perhaps till I am (if I shall ever be) at ease with it.[1]

In another letter he expressed his interest in current politics:

> Politics are amusing and don't take much of my time.... In the senate I speak as little upon politics as is possible, reserving myself for things I understand.[2]

Though Yeats liked being a senator and enjoyed the position, life was not that smooth. After Griffith's death and Collins's assassination, the government was headed by William Cosgrave, one of the Easter Rising leaders, like De Valera and Con Markiewicz. He showed unexpected talent as an administrator. Kevin O'Higgins, who replaced Collins, proved to be "strong man" of the government. He was ably supported by Richard Mulachy in resisting the republicans. The civil war that ensued made the life of the senators perilous. The republicans occasionally fired at the senators and ministers. Yeats's house too was fired upon, which caused two bullet holes in his windows. It is difficult to say if it was a deliberate attack or chance firing.

While in the senate, Yeats systematised his political ideas. But in his speeches he was more a poet than a politician. In fairness to him it can be said that in his speeches he was more concerned with the welfare of the entire nation and much more advanced in his ideas than any other politicians of his time.

Besides, his senate speeches are important for a literary critic because they throw light on some of the important poems he wrote during this period. Earlier Yeats had read Gentile's *The Reformation of Education* and the philosophical works of Berkeley. In one of his senate speeches he said that it was important that education should be imparted in the Italian way because the Italian Gentile was an intellectual descendant of Berkeley and Burke:

> Indeed, the whole curriculum of a school be as it were one lesson and not a mass of unrelated topics. I recommend Irish teachers to study the attempt now being made in Italy, under the influence of their Minister of Education, the philosopher Gentile, the most profound disciple of our own Berkeley, to so correlate all subjects to study. I would have such religion, Catholic or Protestant, so taught that permeate the whole school life...that it may not be abstract and that it may be part of history and life itself, a part, as it were, of the foliage of Burke's tree.[3]

Yeats was really delighted when he visited a school run on the Montessori method. He linked his concept of education with his experience in the school in "Among School Children" which, as Professor Donald Torchiana has interpreted, very artistically conveys Yeats's ideas expressed in his famous speech in the senate.[4] The poem's opening lines describe the poet's visit in the capacity of a senator, his questions, the teacher's replies, his observation and appreciation of the activities of school and small children's inquisitive eyes:

> A walk through the long schoolroom questioning;
> A kind old nun in a white hood replies;
> The children to cipher and to sing,

To study reading-books and histories,
To cut and sew, be neat in everything
In the best modern way—the children's eyes
In momentary wonder stare upon
A sixty-year-old smiling public man.

(*Collected Poems* 242-43)

In the next three stanzas he meditates on Maud Gonne and her statue. The statue represents her old age—"Hollow of cheek as though it drank the wind/And took a mess of shadows for its meat?"—but he, after seeing the young children, remembers Maud in her childhood when she "had that colour upon cheek or hair." The change is great and painful too. He differed with her on many points and though he and she were not of the same mind they complemented each other:

...it seemed that our two natures blent
Into a sphere from youthful sympathy
Or else, to alter Plato's parable,
Into the yolk and white of the one shell.

(*C.P.* 243)

But now he, too, is changed and is not what he was. In the sixth stanza the main question is asked: Did any mother think that the newly born child would develop into a scarecrow? It is on the basis of this question, the neglect of the body, that he rejects Plato. He rejects Aristotle for his neglect of the spirit:

Plato thought nature but a spume that plays
Upon a ghostly paradigm of things;
Solider Aristotle played the taws*
Upon the bottom of a king of kings;
World-famous golden-thighed Pythagoras
Fingered upon a fiddle-stick or strings
What a star sang and careless Muses heard
Old clothes upon old sticks to scare a bind.

(*C.P.* 244)

* The word "taws" created a controversy over its meaning, (see G.S. Fraser, *Vision and Rhetoric* pp. 73-6). But Yeats himself has given the meaning in his letter to Olivia Shakespear: "Here is a fragment of my last curse upon old age. It means that even the greatest men are owls, scarecrows, by the time their fame has come. Aristotle, remember, was Alexander's tutor, hence the taws (form of birch), *The Letters of W.B. Yeats,* 719.

In the essay "The Child and the State" Yeats wrote:

> These artists have said: "Do not put scholars to draw from Greek or Roman casts until they have first drawn from life; only when they have drawn from life can they understand the cast."[5]

In the same essay, a little later, he advised educationists to save children from abstraction:

> Let the child go its own way when maturity comes, but it is our business that it has something of that whole inheritance, and not as a mere thought, an abstract thing like those Gaeco-Roman casts upon the shelves in the art-schools, but as a part of emotional life.[6]

Both these passages explain the references to Plato, Aristotle and Pythagoras. Yeats's idea of education is that it should make a balance between the body and the soul. This idea is expressed in the beautiful images of the chestnut tree and the dancer:

> Labour is blossoming or dancing where
> The beauty is not bruised to pleasure soul,
> Nor beauty born out of its own despair
> Nor blear eyed wisdom out of midnight oil
> O'chestnut tree, great-rooted blossomer
> Are you the leaf, the blossom or the bole
> O body swayed to music, O brightening glance,
> How can we know the dancer from the dance?
>
> (*C.P.* 244-45)

Yeats's speech in the senate illuminates this stanza, especially the last four lines:

> I would like to suggest another principle, that the child itself must be the end in education: It is a curious thing how many times the education of Europe has drifted into error. For two or three centuries people thought that their various religious systems were more important than the child. In the modern world the tendency is to think of the nation; that it is more important than the child.... There is a tendency to subordinate the child to the idea of the nation.... We should always see that the child is the object and not any of our special purpose.[7]

That the tree is the nation is the idea propounded by Burke. In the previously referred to essay "The Child and the State" Yeats wrote:

> Berkeley proved that the world was a vision, and Burke that the State was a tree, no mechanism to be pulled in pieces and put up again; but an oak tree that had grown through centuries.[8]

The idea in the concluding passage is that the aim of education is no doubt to keep a balance between the body and the soul, beauty and wisdom but also to maintain a balance between the state and the child. The chestnut tree is the State and children are its foliage and so are its inseparable and vital part. As we cannot say whether a tree is the root or trunk or the leaves, likewise the state cannot be recognized by its parts; it is a whole which is more than the sum total of its parts and yet without parts it has no existence at all. "Among School Children" however cannot be limited to the interpretation that it is merely a verse form of Yeats's senate speech and the article "The Child and the State." It is a poem, no doubt, inspired by his visit to schools in the capacity of a senator but it is also that it embodies Yeats's philosophy of life, and education is a means to make life better. The poem is artistically perfect. It is the dialectic of the conflicting emotions and their resolution to a higher synthesis that makes its structure an organic whole. The first stanza (lexia in Barthes' terminology) initiates the action—the senator's admiration of the children's activities and their wonder at the sixty year old smiling public man. The second stanza runs counter to it where the senator is the sole actant observing the Ledean body (Maud Gonne), cheeks hollow because of old age and thinking of the past days when she was young and full of beauty. The third stanza is the progression of the first stanza; Maud is remembered as a child in all her innocent beauty. The fourth stanza brings him back from the past and he sees her floating image. Now he cannot but smile ironically at the present condition of once a beautiful body. The fifth stanza is a reflection on the decay of body in old age and poses the problem of transitoriness of beauty. The sixth stanza rejects all the Greek teachers. The seventh stanza expresses the poet's anguish at man's plight. It is only in the last stanza that the antinomies of body and soul, and beauty and wisdom are resolved in the image of the chestnut tree, and the dancer in action. We at once realise at the end that the poem is structured in such a way as to give us a comprehensive idea of Yeats's concept of education and the unity of being, the former a means for the latter which is the end.

Yeats was seriously concerned with the all round development of Children. He wanted them to grow to perfection and achieve Unity of Being. Even though he favoured aristocracy and aristocratic ideals, he loved children of all classes. He appealed to the Irish-Americans to help poor children to receive better education:

> Large sums of money have been sent to Ireland for political ends, and rich Irish-Americans have largely contributed, and we all hope, I think, that there is no further need for the money. If societies like this interest themselves in Irish education and spread this interest among the Irish educated classes everywhere, money may be sent to us to cheapen the price of school-books for the poor, or to clothe the poorer children, or to make the school building pleasanter to a child's eyes, or in some other way to prepare for an Ireland that will be healthy, vigorous, orderly, and above all, happy.[9]

Yeats's speech on divorce was a historic one. He spoke against the proposals to impose the Roman Catholic view of marriage and divorce on the whole state:

> I think it is tragic that within three years of this country gaining independence we should be discussing a measure which a minority of this nation considers to be grossly impressive. I am proud to consider myself a typical man of that minority.[10]

The poem "The Three Monuments" written shortly after this speech, hints in a bitter manner, at the private lives of the three great Irish leaders—Nelson, O'Connell and Parnell whose statues are at the public places—that they had gone against the Catholic view of marriage and divorce:

And all the popular statesmen say
That purity built up the state
And after kept it from decay;
Admonish us to cling to that
And let all base ambition be,
For intellect would make us proud
And pride bring in impurity:
The three old rascals laugh aloud.* (*C.P.* 256)

In the capacity of senator Yeats suggested some of the ministers the best way to end the Civil War. He said that some effort should be made to revise the Treaty to enable De Valera to enter the Dail without loss of principle. He made private efforts also to remove the Oath of Allegiance by negotiation because it was the greatest obstacle in the unity of the Treaty and Anti-Treaty groups and restoration of peace in Ireland. But Cosgrave and his government did not pay serious attention to Yeats's plan. This proved fatal for his government. J. Hone comments in the footnote on page 354 of his biography of the poet:

> If Mr. Cosgrave's Government had adopted Yeats's suggestion it might still be in power. Its opponents subsequently gained a good deal of support from people who believed that negotiations could easily be started with the Imperial Government which would result in the elimination of the Oath.[11]

Kevin O'Higgins's murder on 10 July, 1927 was a great shock to Yeats. Higgins who had succeeded Collins as Vice-President and Minister of Justice, was a strong man and Yeats admired him greatly. He wrote to Olivia Shakespeare:

> The murder of O'Higgins was no mere public event to us. He was our personal friend, as well as the one strong intellect in Irish public life and then too his pretty wife was our friend.[12] He wrote the poem "Death" on O'Higgins. But

* "I have said that this is a tolerant country, yet, remembering that we have in our principal streets certain monuments, I feel it necessary to say that it would be wiser if I had said this country is hesitating.

I have no doubt whatever that, when the iceberg melts, it will become an exceedingly tolerant country. The monuments are on the whole encouraging. I am thinking of O'Connell, Parnell and Nelson." *The Senate Speeches*, 97.

this poem is neither an elegy nor an outburst of anger; it is a philosophical poem that praises O'Higgins's fortitude. It consoles all those who work for a noble cause or, at least, for their principles without fear for death:

A great man in his pride
Confronting murderous men
Casts derision upon
Supersession of breath;
He knows death to the bone—
He has created death. (*C.P.* 264)

The last line invites a comparison with Donne's sonnet ending with "Death thou shalt die." Like Donne Yeats confronts death, but while Donne's approach is religious and ratiocinative, Yeats's approach is heroic and intuitive:

II

Before his retirement from the senate Yeats wrote to Olivia Shakespeare:

> Once out of the senate—my time is up in September—and, in obedience to the doctors, out of all public work, there is no reason for more than three months of Dublin—where the Abbey is the one work I cannot wholly abandon. Once out of Dublin bitterness I can find some measure of sweetness and of light, as befits old age.[13]

Retiring from the senate the busied himself in writing poetry and reading books on history and philosophy, for the revision of *A Vision*:

A Vision, despite its esotericism and bizarre signs and symbols, is not unreadable. It is of use to the scholars and critics of Yeats not only for its "metaphors for poetry," as Yeats's "instructors" professed, but also for Yeats's interpretation of history and the place of unity of being and unity of culture in it. The first three chapters deal with the unity of being.

Man's soul, like the twenty-eight phases of the moon, has twenty-eight incarnations. The circle consisting of the twenty-eight incarnations is divided into two halves ("tinctures"). The first half is called the "primary tincture" and it covers phases one to seven and phases twenty-three to twenty-eight; the second half, the "antithetical tincture" covers the other remaining phases. The "primary tincture" is objective and the "antithetical tincture" is subjective. The fifteenth phase is the state of the unity of being but it does not exist in the bodily form, being the superhuman incarnation.

In the last two chapters Yeats interprets the flux and influx of history from the beginning of the Greek civilization to the present age. He divides the Great Year, as conceived by ancient astrologers, into thirteen "lesser periods" each consisting of two milleniums, the first antithetical and the second primary. The antithetical is subjective and the primary objective. Yeats explains his concept of the Great Year:

> 'By common consent men measure the year,' wrote Cicero, 'by the return of the sun, or in other words by the revolution of one star. But when the whole of the constellations shall return to the positions from which they once set forth, thus after a long interval remaking the first map of the heavens, that may indeed be called the Great Year in which I searce dare say how many are the generations of men. But the Great or Greatest Year was something divided into lesser periods by the return of a planet or of all the planets to some original position.[14]

Each "lesser period" is a wheel and the milleniums, too, though a part of the "lesser period" are independent wheels in themselves. "One must bear in mind," writes Yeats:

> that the Christian Era, like two thousand years, let us say, that went before it, is an entire wheel and each half of it an entire wheel, that each half when it comes to its 28th Phase reaches the 15th Phase or the 8th Phase of the entire era.[15]

A civilization comes to its end after two thousand years. The older civilization of Babylon died and a new civilization, the Greek civilization, took its place. The Greek civilization began with the anunciation of Leda. After two thousand years began the Christian era with the anunciation of Mary. It follows, then, that the phase fifteeen (the state of the unity of being and the unity of culture) occurred twice only in the recorded history of civilization. First it occurred in the time of Pythagoras.* The unity of culture was achieved for the second time in the reign of Justinian, and in Ireland in the eighteenth century. Yeats describes in detail, the time when the unity of culture was achieved in Byzantium:

> I think that in early Byzantium, may be never before or since in recorded history, religious, aesthetic and practical life were one, that architect and artificers—though not, it may be, poets of language had been the instrument of controversy and must have grown abstract—spoke to the multitude and the few alike. The painter, the mosaic worker, the worker in gold and silver, the illuminator of sacred books, were almost impersonal perhaps without the consciousness of individual design, absorbed in their subject-matter and that the vision of a whole people...and this vision, this proclamation of their invisible master, had the Greek nobility.[16]

A little later he says:

> If I were left to myself I could make Phase 15 coincide with Justinian's reign, that great age of building in which one may conclude Byzantine art was perfected.[17]

Yeats defines the unity of culture as a unified society in which the artists strive to achieve the unity of being, the central image which binds the nations, individuals and civilizations together. The artist, in the fifteenth phase, absorbs himself in the work of art and in the vision of the whole people. The creation of great works of art was possible in the times of Pythagoras and Justinian when artists could express through their art the vision of the whole people.

But the gyres run on. After phase 15, the period of beauty, come phases sixteen, seventeen and so on. The cycle of history reaches phase 28 when a civilization reaches its end and soon after it there is the birth of a new civilization. The present Christian civilization, too, Yeats feels, has entered its twenty

---

* "There are moments when I am certain that art must accept those Greek proportions which carry into plastic art the Pythagorean numbers, those faces which are divine because all there is empty and measured." Explorations, 451.

second phase. Yeats's observations are quite interesting and they have much relevance to his political and prophetic poems:

> The period from 1875 to 1927 (Phase 22—in some countries and in some forms of thought the Phase runs from 1815 to 1927) is like that from 1250 to 1300 (Phase 8) a period of abstraction and like it also in that it is preceded and followed by abstraction. Phase 8 was preceded by the Schoolmen and followed by legalists and inquisitors, and Phase 22 was preceded by the great popularisers of physical science and economic science, and will be followed by social movements and applied sciences. Abstraction which began at Phase 19 will end at Phase 25, for these movements and this science will have their object or result the elimination of intellect.[18]

In the final chapter titled "The End of the Cycle" Yeats meditates and turns symbols after symbols to know the future. Since he himself is unable to see the future he doubts the socialistic and communistic prophecies. He then draws himself into the symbol in order to get rid of his memories and find everything in the symbol:

> But nothing comes—though this moment was to reward me for all my toil. Perhaps I am too old. Surely something would have come when I meditated under the direction of the cabalists. What discords will drive Europe to the artificial unity—only dry or drying sticks can be tied into a bundle—which is the decadence of every civilization? How work out upon the phase the gradual coming and increase of the counter-movement, the antithetical multiform influx:
>
> Should Jupiter and Saturn meet,
> O what a crop of mummy wheat!
>
> Then I understand. I have already said all that can be said. The particulars are the work of the *Thirteenth Cone* or cycle which is in every man and called by every man his freedom. Doubtless, for it can do all things and knows all things, it knows what it will do with its own freedom but it has kept the secret.[19]

Yeats's conception of history is not mechanical. It is a mythical interpretation, partly based on Toynbee's notion of history, that considers the movement of history in cycles. But this movement is not automatic. At every critical moment the *Thirteenth Cone*, the individual freedom or freewill plays the vital role and this is why no prophet or seer can predict future convincingly or accurately.

Now the question arises: Can *A Vision* be said to have relevance to Yeats's poetry in general and political poetry in particular? According to T.R. Henn, *A Vision* has interest for three reasons: first, it gives us a good idea of Yeats's interpretation of history, second it is important for the symbolic values Yeats found in the works of artists and third, it provides clues to the writings of his mind.[20] Professor Henn's explanation cannot be challenged. But what he has forgot to refer to is its practical implications whether it presents any solution to the problems of the present time.

In my humble view, *A Vision* first reflects Yeats's attitude to the present age in its relation to the past ages. To him phase 15 is the ideal period in the cyclic history of a civilization. Ireland had phase 15 in the eighteenth century when unity of culture was achieved. After that there was a slow decline in the society. This gradual decline aggrieved him. The worsening situation in Ireland and the rest of the world made him think of phase 28. It also impelled him to ask the question, does every civilization end in a tragic way? The answer, a tentative and not very convincing, is given in the concluding paragraphs of *A Vision* that it is the *Thirteenth Cone* that intervenes. Therefore, the artists, the builders of civilization, should accept the historical process, have trust in individual's freedom, and hope that they will build a new civilization. This is what he says in "Lapis Lazuli." In the third stanza he describes the fall of civilizations:

On their own feet they came, or on shipboard,
Camel-back, horse-back, ass-back, mule-back
Old civilizations put to the sword. (*C.P.* 338)

The situation is really tragic. But the artists must remain gay even when a civilization is going to die. This is because they are the builders:

All things fall and are built again
And those that build them again are gay. (*C.P.* 339)

A Vision, is a mythico-poetical (all myths are poetry) interpretation of history in terms of rise-fall-rise of civilizations and thus it provides a system to Yeats's poetry which deals with the crisis of values and human existence in the troubled political situation of the present age.

III

If history shows that civilizations must die, that with the death of civilization a new civilization is born and that "Everything that man esteems/Endures a moment or a day," what will be the enduring ideals? Yeats's major poems make a serious attempt to establish those enduring ideals; "Sailing to Byzantium," "Byzantium," "Among School Children," "The Double Vision of Michael Roberts" and "The Phases of the Moon" are primarily concerned with the unity being; the poems with tower as a major symbol deal with the unity of culture as their main theme.

"Sailing to Byzantium" is man's journey to Justinian's Byzantium, the Byzantium of the fifteenth phase, when there was the unity of culture at its peak. It is at this place and in this period that the unity of being is possible and the antinomy of body and soul, youth and age and beauty and wisdom is resolved. The last stanza is a perfect rendering of Yeats's aspiration for this status. In "Byzantium" there is the depiction of the unity of being in the third stanza:

Miracle, bird or golden handiwork
More miracle than bird or handiwork,
Planted on the star-lit golden bough,
Can like the cocks of Hades crow,
Or, by the moon embittered, scorn aloud
In glory of changeless metal
Common bird or petal
And all complexities of mire or blood. (*C.P.* 280-81)

In the "Double Vision of Michael Roberts" the images of Buddha, Sphinx and the dancing girl symbolise the unity of being and likewise is the image of the dancer in action—"How can we know the dancer from the dance—in "Among School Children." The same image of the dancer, and this time not of one individual but of a large number of people, dancing on the Emperor's pavement, occurs in the fourth stanza to suggest that when there is the unity culture, all the people of a nation are unified by a single image and attain the unity of being:

> Where blood-begotten spirits come
> And complexities of furies leave
> Dying into a dance,
> An agony of trance
> An agony of flame that cannot singe a sleeve.
>
> (*C.P.* 281)

The Irish people, especially the aristocratic heroes, achieved unity of being in the eighteenth century when the nation was passing through phase 15 and when there was the reign of the unity of culture. Naturally Yeats has based his poetry on the aristocratic ideals for the revival of the unity of culture. The symbol tower embodies both the ancient Irish tradition and the aristocracy. In the poem "To Be Carved On A Stone At Thoor Ballylee" he uses the symbol tower to represent the aristocratic tradition:

> I the poet William Yeats
> With old mill boards and sea-green slates,
> And smithy work from the Gort Forge,
> Restore this tower for my wife George,
> And may these characters remain
> When all is ruin once again. (*C.P.* 216)

The meaning of the symbol is further expanded in the famous poem "The Tower" where he describes the passionate subjective heroic people, maintaining and enriching the glorious ancient tradition, with the assertion that in spite of the prevailing chaos and the bleak future they will carry it on undaunted. The third section is a bold defence and emphatic assertion of this ancient tradition and the faith that the younger generation will not betray the nation:

> I have both faith and pride
> To young upstanding men
> Climbing the mountain-side
> That under bursting dawn
> They may drop a fly; (*C.P.* 224)

In "Blood and the Moon" there is a greater defence of the "tower." In the first seven lines of Section I Yeats is quite specific in defining it that it is a symbol of the ancient Irish race, a race that defended the cause of Ireland by its heroic sacrifices. But the next five lines make the symbol more complex; we begin to feel that the "tower" represents all that Yeats considers valuable and precious. The symbol goes on expanding and growing complex in Section II where it embodies the unity of culture in phase 15 in Babylon and Alexandria:

> Alexandria was a beacon tower, and Babylon's
> An image of the moving heavens, a log-book of the
> sun's journey and the moon's. (*C.P.* 268)

In the next line Yeats refers to Shelley who, in his opinion, called towers as "thought's crowned powers." And then follows the proud declaration:

> I declare this tower is my symbol; I declare
> This winding, gyring, spiring treadmill of a stair is
> my ancestral stair;
> That Goldsmith and the Dean, Berkeley and Burke have
> travelled there. (*C.P.* 268)

Swift, Goldsmith, Burke and Berkeley were not considered a part of the Irish tradition in his early writings, but now they are all counted as creators of the true Irish philosophy, the "thought's crowned powers," the best products of the eighteenth century. Dean Swift's scorn for the populous, Goldsmith's love of humanity, Burke's concept that the state is a tree and Berkeley's philosophy that the world is a dream—all he comes to believe have created the philosophic tradition of Ireland. Earlier in "The Tower" he had written:

> And I declare my faith:
> I mock Plotinus' thought
> And cry in Plato's teeth,
> Death and life were not
> Till man made up the whole. (*C.P.* 223)

Now he finds the foundation of his faith in Berkeley, Burke and Gentile, the Italian Philosopher whom he considers a disciple of Berkeley. The significance of the symbol "tower" does not end here. That it resolves the antinomy of wisdom and power is expressed in the image of the tower basking in the purity of the unclouded moon. Blood which is the symbol of life on this earth and also of power has not been able to stain the tower. For Yeats, the earthly life is important but it is not complete in itself; life can be made perfect by balancing both the material and spiritual sides. He, like other major poets, is in quest of permanence but this permanence he does not seek in a straight way, denying the body for soul, beauty for wisdom, knowledge for power and youth for age. In the fifteenth phase he envisages all antinomies, all the four faculties—will, mask, creative mind and body of fate—are in complete unison. Seen in this way the tower symbolises the unity of culture where unity of being is possible.

The poems Yeats wrote during the period he was a senator are the best fruit of his political, philosophical and occultist ideas, all the three forged together for the attainment of unity of culture and unity of being. His ideas and endeavours may sound impractical and his conviction that the state should be ruled by the best way appear a little too absurd in our age of democracy but what is more important for us to realize is the fact that he wanted to make Ireland philosophically and culturally superior. In his early life he laid more emphasis on culture but after becoming a senator he tried to understand the political situation of the world in general and of Ireland in particular by a philosophical system of his own. He sincerely felt that a nation without a philosophy could not make a headway when it was facing a great challenge nor could fathers say to their children what their country excelled in.*

In the senate Yeats spoke as a public man representing the class he belonged to but, sitting in Thoor Ballylee he reflected

---

* Once Yeats's son, Michael, asked his teacher what Ireland excelled in. The teacher could not reply. Yeats, too, did not know the answer at that time. But when he sat to write in his diary he realised that he would say these words to his son.

"I may suggest to him if I live long enough, that the thought of Swift, enlarged and enriched by Burke, saddled and bitted reality and that materialism was hamstrung by Berkeley, and ancient wisdom brought back; that modern Europe has known no men more powerful...." Quoted by John Unterecker, *A Reader's Guide to W.B. Yeats,* 206.

on the nation and entire humanity and conceived of a world where the unity of culture and the unity of being were possible.

REFERENCES

1. A. Wade, ed., *The Letters of W.B. Yeats,* 694.
2. *Ibid.,* 704.
3. D. Pearce, ed., *The Senate Speeches,* 173-74.
4. Donald Torchiana, "Among School Children: The Irish Spirit *is Excited Reverie,* 140.
5. John P. Frayne, *Uncollected Prose By W.B. Yeats,* Vol. II, 457.
6. *Ibid.,* 460.
7. Donald R. Pearce, ed., *The Senate Speeches,* 111-12.
8. John P. Frayne, *Uncollected Prose By W.B. Yeats,* Vol. II, 459.
9. *Ibid.,* 461.
10. Donald R. Pearce, ed., *The Senate Speeches,* 96.
11. J. Hone, *W.B. Yeats 1865-1939,* 354.
12. A. Wade, ed., *The Letters of W.B. Yeats,* 726.
13. *Ibid.,* 737.
14. *A Vision,* 245-46.
15. *Ibid.,* 267.
16. *Ibid.,* 279-80.
17. *Ibid.,* 281.
18. *Ibid.,* 299.
19. *Ibid.,* 301-02.
20. T.R. Henn, *The Lonely Tower,* 191-92.

7

Swift and Fascism

I

Yeats studied the works of Swift, Berkeley, Burke and Gentile while he was revising the text of *A Vision*. He arrived at the conclusion that Gentile had derived many of his ideas from Berkeley. Writing to Hone he observed:

> You have set Berkeley in his first world and made him amusing, animated and intelligible. He is of the utmost importance to the Ireland that is coming into existence, as I hope to show in my introduction. I want Protestant Ireland to base some vital part of its culture upon Burke, Swift and Berkeley.* Rossi's help is of course of first importance, Gentile and other Italian philosophers found themselves on Berkeley, and Rossi has the further advantage of being an authority on Berkeley's immediate predecessors and contemporaries.[1]

The letter shows that after retirement from the senate Yeats did not cut himself off from current politics; on the other hand he was still thinking of reviving the golden period of Ireland. He wrote to Lady Gregory:

> I want to bring out a book of four plays called 'My Wheels and Butterflies'—the wheels are the four introductions. Dublin is said to be full of little societies meeting in cellars and garrets, so I shall put this rhyme on the leaf:
>
> To Cellar and Garret
> A wheel I send

* "...these two images, standing and sounding together, Swift and Berkeley, concern all those who feel a responsibility for the thought of modern Ireland that can take away their sleep." *Essays and Introductions,* 397.

> But every butterfly
> To a friend.

The 'wheels' are addressed to Ireland mainly—a scheme of intellectual nationalism.[2]

The "Introduction" to the play *The Words Upon The Window-Pane*, one of the wheels, is largely a scheme of intellectual nationalism. It begins with a reference to the clubs in Dublin, which held meetings in cellars and garrets and passed resolutions against censorship. Yeats remembers the days after Parnell's fall when the number of such clubs was much larger. Now, he says that time has come to take decision on the future of Ireland:

> Hitherto we have walked the road, but now we have shut the door and turned up the lamp. What shall occupy our imagination? We must, I think, decide upon these three ideas of national life; that of Swift; that of a great Italian of his day* that of modern England. If the Garrets and Cellars listen I may throw light upon the matter, and I hope if all the time I seem thinking of something else I shall be forgiven. I must speak of things that come out of the common consciousness, where every thought is like a bell with many echoes.[3]

This passage quoted from the "Introduction" to *Words Upon The Window-Pane*, a play on Jonathan Swift, throws light on the functioning of Yeats's as does the entry in his diary of 1930. In fact the "Introduction" provides a summary of his political philosophy and it should be read along with *A Vision*. In the diary of 1930 he writes:

> I would found literature on three things which Kant thought we must postulate to make life livable—Freedom, God, Immortality.[4]

A little later he links these three with the idea of the state:

> An idea of the State which is not a preparation for those three convictions, a State founded on economics alone, would be a prison house. A State must be like a Chartres Cathedral for the glory of God and the soul. It exists for

* Yeats is referring to Baldassare Castiglione, author of *The Courtier*.

> the sake of the virtues and must pay their price. The uneconomic leisure of scholars, monks and women gave us truth, sanctity, and manners. Free power is not the denial of that past but such a conflagration or integration of that past that it can be grasped in a single thought.[5]

He rejects the idea that economics is the only basis of a state; for him the uneconomic activities are equally important. In other words cultural and spiritual activities which do not produce wealth are equally important and for this freedom, God and immortality must be our convictions. He writes:

> When I speak of the three convictions and of the idea of the State I do not mean any metaphysical or economic theory. That belief which I call free power is free because we cannot distinguish between the things believed in and the beliefs, it is something forced on us bit by bit; as it liberates our energies we sink in on truth.[6]

He, then, advises his countrymen to follow the eighteenth century heroes who were a great beauty and then criticises O'Connell and his people:

> The great men of the eighteenth century were that beauty (naked beauty displayed); Parnell had something of it, O'Leary something, but what have O'Connell and all his seed, breed, and generation but a roaring machine?[7]

Swift, Burke and Berkeley, unified Ireland in the eighteenth century; now it is high time to unify the divided nation by following this philosophy and ideals. He advises:

> Preserve that which is living and help the two Irelands, Gaelic Ireland and Anglo-Ireland,* so to unite that neither shall shed its pride. Study the great problems of the world, as they have been lived in our scenery, the rebirth of European spirituality in the mind of Berkeley, the restoration of European order in the mind of Burke. Every nation is the whole world in a mirror, and our mirror has twice been very bright and clear. Do not be afraid to boast so long as the boast lays burdens on the boaster. Study the educational system of Italy, the creation of the philosopher

---

* Yeats and many of the patriots were Anglo-Irish.

> Gentile, where even religion is studied not in the abstract but in the minds and lives of Italian saints and thinkers, it becomes at once part of Italian history.[8]

The ideas expressed in the diary of 1930 are closely related to the "Introduction." He refers to Swift's ideas expressed in *Discourse of the Contests and Dissensions Between the Nobles and the Commons in Athens and Rome,* a pamphlet written for the purpose of warning the Tory opposition against the impeachment of ministers. After this Yeats explains his concept of the state, which is derived mainly from the *Discourse.* I quote the relevant part:

> All states depend for their health upon a right balance between the One, the Few and the Many. The One is the executive, which may in fact be more than one—the Roman republic had two consuls—but must for the sake of rapid decision be as few as possible; the Few are those who through the possession of heredity, wealth or great personal gifts come to identify their lives with the life of the State, whereas the lives and ambitions of the Many are private. The Many do their day's work well, and so far from copying even the wisest of their neighbours, affect "a singularity" in action and in thought; but set them to the work of the State and every man Jack is "listed in a party," becomes the fanatical follower of men whose characters he knows next to nothing, and from that day on puts nothing into his mouth that some other man has not already chewed and digested. And furthermore, from the moment of enlistment thinks himself above other men and struggles for power until all is in confusion. I divine an Irish hatred of abstraction likewise expressed by that fable of Gulliver among the inventors and men of science, by Berkeley in his *Common-Place Book,* by Goldsmith in the satire of *The Good Natured Man,* in the picturesque minute observation of *The Deserted Village,* and by Burke in his attack upon mathematical democracy. Swift enforced his moral by proving that Rome and Greece were destroyed by the war of the Many upon the Few; in Rome, where the Few had kept their class organization, it was a war of classes, in Greece, where they had not, war upon character and genius.[9]

Here, Yeats envisages after Swift that the government should be run by the One who is to be advised and supported by the Few (aristocracy) and liberty depends upon the balance between the One (Executive), the Few (aristocracy) and the Many (peasantry).[10] For Yeats, Swift was a great champion of liberty and he deprecated any kind of conflict between the three classes. Comparing Giambdistta Vico's ideas with those of Swift, he writes:

> Swift, a practical politician in everything he wrote, ascribed its (civilization's) rise and fall to virtues and vices all could understand, whereas the philosophical Vico ascribed them to 'the rhythm of the elemental forms of the mind,' a new idea that would dominate philosophy.[11]

And a little later he, in his own way, finds a similarity between Sorel, Marx and Swift:

> Both Sorel and Marx, their eyes more Swift's than Vico's, have preached a return to a primeval state, a beating of all down into a single class that a new civilization may arise with its Few, its Many, and its One.[12]

We all know that Marx never thought of such a civilization; he envisioned a classless society in which there would not be exploitation of people on the basis of man-made laws. Yeats certainly misinterprets him but when he associates Marx with Swift he surely thinks of a society free from all kinds of exploitation. He further argues that Swift's notion of liberty is positive:

> Liberty depended upon a balance within the State like that of the 'humours' in a human body, or like that 'unity of being' Dante compared to a perfectly proportioned human body, and for its sake Swift was prepared to sacrifice what seems to be the modern liberty itself.[13]

For Yeats, perfect liberty reigned in Ireland in the eighteenth century, when balance between the One (executive), the Few (aristocracy) and the Many (peasantry) was maintained. But this state of liberty did not last long as, later on, a new class, the middle class, emerged and began to dominate the Irish scene. If liberty is to be achieved, Yeats argues, there is the necessity to reverse the process of progression.

"The Seven Sages" glorifies the eighteenth century Ireland and its champions of liberty. The sages proudly refer to the friendship of their ancestors with Swift, Burke, Goldsmith, Stella and Berkeley who was Bishop of Cloyne:

The First, My great-grandfather spoke to Edmund Burke
In Grattan's house.
The Second, My great-grandfather shared
A pot-house bench with Oliver Goldsmith once.
The Third, My great-grandfather talked of music,
Drank tar-water with the Bishop of Cloyne.
The Fourth, But mine saw Stella once.

[*Collected Poems* 271-72]

The Sixth sage praises them because they were all subjective minds and represented the true Irish tradition and hated whiggery:

Whether they knew or not
Goldsmith and Burke, Swift and the Bishop of Cloyne
All hated whiggery; but what is whiggery?
A levelling, rancorous, rational sort of mind
That never looked out of the eye of saint
Or out of a drunkard's eye. (*C.P.* 272)

The next speech of the first sage reveals Yeat's broad mind. We all know that Burke was a champion of liberty and he spoke for the freedom of America in the British Parliament and moved impeachment against Warren Hastings for exploiting Indians. By supporting Burke, Yeats speaks for the liberty of all the countries of the world:

American colonies, Ireland, France and India
Harried, and Burke's great melody against it. (*C.P.* 272)

We can safely say that Yeat's political philosophy has its source in the writings of Swift, Burke, Berkeley and Goldsmith who were all humanitarians and who had an international outlook. However, it is Swift who is the greatest influence on the poet:

> But now I read Swift for months together, Burke and Berkeley less often but always with excitement, and Goldsmith lures and waits. I collect materials for my

> thought and work, for some identification of my beliefs with the nation itself, I seek an image of the modern mind's discovery of itself, of its own permanent form, in that one Irish century that escaped from darkness and confusion.[14]

For Yeats, Swift was the ideal eighteenth century Irish who almost achieved the unity of being. The following passage again from the "Introduction" tells us how deeply he was influenced by Swift in the thirties:

> Swift haunts me; he is always just round the next corner. Sometimes it is a thought of my great-great grandmother, a friend of that Archbishop King who sent him to England about the 'First Fruits,' sometimes it is saint Patrick's, where I have gone to wander and meditate, that brings him to mind, sometimes I remember something harsh in O'Leary or in Taylor, or in the public speech of our statesmen, that reminds me by its style of his verse or prose. Did he not speak, perhaps, with just such an intonation?[15]

And a little later, he pays a glowing tribute to the greater writer:

> I remember the shudder in my spine when Mr. Patrick Campbell said, speaking words Hofmannsthal put into the mouth of Electra, 'I too am of that ancient race':
>
> Swift has sailed into his rest.*
> Savage indignation there
> Cannot lacerate his breast
> Imitate him if you dare
> World-besotted traveller; he
> Served human liberty.[16]

It is under the influence of Swift that Yeats wrote the poem "Remorse for Intemperate speech." The Irish indignation that lacerated Swift heart, lacerates Yeat's too. He says that he wanted to speak softly and gently and soothen his hatred for England as a nation but he finds it impossible to do so as he is a descendant of the Dean:

> I sought my betters, though in each
> Fine manners, liberal speech

* This poem is included in *Collected Poems*, 277, with the title "Swift's Epitaph."

Turn hatred into a sport
Nothing said or done can reach.
My fanatic heart. (*C.P.* 288)

The reason for his intemperate language and "fanatic heart" is he explains in the concluding stanza of the poem, that he has inherited fanaticism from his ancestors (Swift is one of them):

Out of Ireland have we come
Great hatred, little room
Maimed us at the start
I carry from my mother's womb
A fanatic heart. (*C.P.* 288)

"Parnell's Funeral" is equally Swiftian. Here he deplores the lack of Parnell's heroic character in the leaders of nineteen-thirties. Describing the great leader's funeral* as narrated by Maud Gonne, he refers to the myth of *The Woman and The Archer*. The first stanza shows the relation between the death of Parnell and the slaying of the Tree-spirit** or Apollo:

Under the great comedian's tomb the crowd
A bundle of tempestuous cloud is blown
About the sky; where that is clear of cloud
Brightness remains: a brighter star shoots down;
What shudder runs through all that animal blood?
What is this sacrifice? Can someone there
Recall the Cretan barb that pierced a star? (*C.P.* 319)

The next stanza describes the ritual:

Rich foliage that the starlight glittered throng!
A frenzied crowd, and where the branches sprang
A beautiful seated boy; a sacred bow;
A woman, and an arrow on a string;
A pierced boy; image of a star laid low
That woman, the Great Mother imaging
Cut out his heart.... (*C.P.* 319)

The slain boy, like the slain vegetation God in *The Waste Land* is reborn. The funeral of Parnell (which coincided with the

* Maud Gonne told Yeats, who did not attend Parnell's funeral, that when his body was being laid down a bright star shot in the sky in the broad day light.

** The myth of the Tree-spirit is analysed in *The Golden Bough*.

shooting of a star) is a ritual—"an age is the reversal of an age"—but the difference is that Parnell's soul, unlike that of the slain God, is not going to be born again. The reason is that the present crowd is in "popular rage" and is not possessed by frenzy as is the crowd of the myth:

> What matter for the scene, the scene once gone:
> It had not touched our lives. But popular rage
> *Hysterica passio* dragged this quarry down
> None shared our guilt, nor did we play a part
> Upon a painted stage when we devoured his heart.
> (*C.P.* 320)

Yeats looks at Parnell's successors and finds that they lack his nobility and heroism. If De Valera* had eaten Parnell's heart (meaning if he had inherited Parnell's noble and heroic character) Ireland would not have suffered disintegration:

> Had de Valera eaten Parnell's heart the land's
> No loose-lipped demagogue had won the day.
> No civil rancour torn the land apart. (*C.P.* 320)

In the same vein he accuses Cosgrave of timidity:

> Had Cosgrave eaten Parnell's heart the land's
> Imagination had been satisfied,
> Or lacking that, government in such hands,
> O'Higgins its sole statesman had not died. (*C.P.* 320)

Yeats always supported William T. Cosgrave. He did everything

---

* Yeats had an ambivalent attitude to De Valera. One of the heroes of the Easter Rising, he fell in Yeat's eyes when the Civil War broke out; if he wanted the bloodshed on both sides could be prevented. Hone quotes Yeats's reaction to a speech of De Valera:

> "A living argument rather a living man. All propaganda, no human life, but not bitter or hysterical or unjust. I judged him persistent, being both patient and energetic, but that he will fail through not having enough life as to judge the human life in others. He will ask too much of everyone and will ask it without charm. He will be pushed aside by others."

Hone soon adds in the footnote:

> "When he met De Valera some years later he, like most others, found a charm in the personal contact that did not appear in the speeches." Joseph Hone, *W.B. Yeats*, 323.

However, Yeats never pardoned De Valera for the Civil War.

for Cosgrave in the 1932 election.* But he never considered him a true successor of Parnell, nor did he pardon him for his failure in protecting O'Higgins's life.

Eoin O'Duffy whose Blue Shirts Movement had attracted him greatly in 1933 fails to reach the height of a great leader:

> Had even O'Duffy—but I name no more—
> Their school a crowd, his master a solitude. (*C.P.* 320)

The last two lines express Yeats's admiration for Swift's political ideas and exhort the Irish people to follow his example as Parnell did:

> Through Jonathan Swift's dark grove he passed and there
> Plucked bitter wisdom that enriched his blood:
> (*C.P.* 320)

The 1932 election result saddened Yeats. In his eyes Cosgrave was far better than De Valera. So, when the Blue Shirts Movement, a fascist organization, started under the leadership of O'Duffy, he hailed it with great enthusiasm. He wrote to Olivia Shakespeare:

> Politics are growing heroic. De Valera has forced political thought to face the most fundamental issues. A Fascist opposition (Blue Shirt Movement) is forming behind to be ready should some tragic situation develop. I find myself constantly urging the despotic rule of the educated classes as the only end to our troubles. (Let all this sleep in your ear).... Our chosen colour is blue, and the blue shirts are marching about all over the country, and their organizer tells me that it was my suggestion—a suggestion I have entirely forgotten—that made them select for their flag a red St. Paul's cross on a blue ground—all I can remember is that I have always denounced green and commended blue (the colour of my early book covers).[17]

---

* Yeats wrote the article "Ireland, 1921-31" where he praised the Cosgrave government of the economic development of the country:

> "When I think of the legislation of those ten years I think first of the roads which have brought lorry and bus, the newspaper, and here and there books, to remote villages; then of the electrical works at Adnacrusha. These works are successful; the demand has exceeded the prophecy of the Minister." *Uncollected Prose*, Vol. II, 488. In the same article he praised the government for the increase in the cultural activities in Ireland.

The next letter describes his meeting with O'Duffy:

> The great secret is out—a convention of blue shirts—National Guards—have received their new leader with the Fascist salute and the new leader announces reform of parliament as his business.
>
> When I wrote to you, the Fascist organizer of the blue shirts had told me that he was about to bring to see me the man he had selected for leader that I might talk my anti-democratic philosophy. I was ready, for I had just rewritten for the seventh time the part of *A Vision* that deals with the future. The leader turned out to be general O' Duffy, head of the Irish police for twelve years, and a famous organizer...Italy, Poland, Germany, then perhaps Ireland. Doubtless I hate it (though not so much as I hate Irish democracy) but it is September and we must not behave like the gay young sparks of May or June.[18]

Yeats hailed the Blue Shirts Movement with great enthusiasm but it was not his ideal. He greeted O'Duffy because he did not like De Valera and William Cosgrave had lost the election. He hoped that fascism would replace Irish democracy of De Valera and revive the spirit of the old heroic Ireland:

> When nations are empty up there at the top,
> When order had weakened or faction is strong,
> Time for us all to pick out a good time,
> Take to the roads and go marching along
> March, march—How does it run?
> O any old words to a tune. (*C.P.* 323)

But this enthusiasm evaporated soon. He soon learnt that fascism was associated with cruelty, tyranny and racism.

It has been customary of critics to ignore Yeats's support of fascism or speak very lightly of it. Professor A.N. Jeffares takes it lightly:

> The question of Yeats's fascism has been raised by several critics, but the essentially Irish trait of using a theory for a plaything must not be forgotten, especially in Yeats's case.[19]

What is objectionable in Jeffares's conclusion is the word "plaything." T.R. Henn is right when he comments:

> I do not excuse the brief association with General O' Duffy's Blue Shirts, except to suggest that he was not alone in believing, at that moment of history, that the discipline fascist theory might impose an order upon a disintegrating world. Though indeed nothing could be farther from Yeats's mind than its violent and suppressive practice.[20]

The letters and the *Diary* written in 1930 reveal the truth that Yeats took fascism and the Blue Shirts Movement seriously. He was full of hope that the movement would revive the old heroic Ireland and O'Duffy would be one of the heroes. Jeffares is confused when he makes distinction between the Yeats of fascism and the "true Yeats."* C.C.O' Brian, too, is off the point when he refutes the arguments of Jeffares, "I cannot see on what grounds," he observes:

> We are to regard the Yeats who began to sneer at the Blue-shirts when they proved a flop, as being more "real" than the Yeats who was excited about them when he thought that they might win. It was the same Yeats, strongly drawn to Fascism, but no lover of hopeless causes.[21]

It is certain that Yeats was not an opportunist as O'Brien considers him to be. He had fought heroically for Parnell, for the Irish Dramatic Movement and for the Hugh Lane pictures. If he were an opportunist, he could easily become a citizen of England and praise the British Crown. If he had sincerely felt that fascism was necessary for Ireland he would have continued to champion its cause as he did for aristocracy. He wrote to Olivia Shakespeare:

> Italy, Poland, Germany, then perhaps Ireland. *Doubtless I shall hate it*** (though not so much as I hate Irish democracy)."

Yeats's infatuation with fascism was serious, no doubt, but not without reservations. He, as the letter shows, hated it but hailed

---

* Commenting on the letter writen on 27 February, 1934, Jeffares writes: "This ironic attitude to the Blue Shirts reveals the *true Yeats*, detached and merely playing with his thoughts, except for the intervals when he wanted to achieve complete directness and accuracy." *W.B. Yeats: Man and the Poet*, 279.

** Italics mine. The letter is already quoted. *Vide infra.*

it because, it was, in his eyes, going to replace De Valera's democracy, the object of greater hatred. He became a supporter of aristocracy with the turn of the century and felt great pain when he saw aristocracy decline. He sincerely felt that art and culture would flourish in aristocracy only. When he started reading philosophy and history for revising *A Vision*, he found that Swift, Berkeley, Burke, Goldsmith, Vico and Gentile all held, more or less similar views on the nature of the state and the liberty of people.* He erroneously concluded that the Blue Shirts Movement was inspired by the philosophy of the mentioned writers. He welcomed the arrival of the movement:

> There is so little in our stocking that we are ready at any moment to turn it inside out, and how can we not feel emulous when we see Hitler juggling with his sausage of stocking. Our chosen colour is blue.... History is very simple—the rule of the many, then the rule of the few, day and night, night and day for ever, while in small disturbed nations day and night race.[22]

He wrote about Eoin O'Duffy that he was striving for the unity of culture in Ireland:

> He seemed to me a plastic man that I could not judge whether he would prove plastic to the opinions of others, obvious political current, or to his own will (unity of being).[23]

Yeats's notion of fascism, we may say, was not the fascism of Hitler, Mussolini or General Franco; it was a kind of staunch nationalism. When he found that it was opposed to human values, he dissociated himself from it. He expressed his disillusionment with the Blue Shirts and fascism in the poem "Church and State," a short poem of two stanzas which are in contrast. The contrast is accentuated by repetition of lines with alteration of a few words. The first stanza is the dream of the future:

> Here is fresh matter poet,
> Matter for old age meet;

---

* Here my aim is not to defend Yeats but to describe the working of Yeats's mind. Yeats was partly wrong in eulogising aristocracy. What is important to know is that Yeats linked fascism with aristocracy.

> Might of the Church and the State,
> Their mobs put under their feet
> O' but heart's wine shall run pure
> Mind's bread grow sweet.

This is the hope Yeats had at the start of the Blue Shirts Movement. But after seeing the ugly face of fascism, he realises the truth and deplores writing the marching songs for the Blue Shirts:

> That were a cowardly song,
> Wander in dreams no more;
> What if the Church and the State
> Are the mob that howls at the door!
> Wine shall run thick to the end,
> Bread taste sour. (*C.P.* 327)

II

Bidding goodbye to fascism Yeats remained silent for sometime and made no comments on the political issues. Perhaps, one important reason was the shock he received from fascism, especially the happenings in Germany and Spain. But he bore the shock well. With a renewed vigour he started writing poems on public events. However, he remained cautious and did not support any political party; he remained rather reserved. When Ethel Mannin requested him to recommend the poet Ossietsky, who was imprisoned in the Nazi camp, for the Nobel Prize, he refused to oblige him and wrote:

> Do not try to make a politician of me, even in Ireland I shall never think I be that again—as my sense of reality deepens, and I think it does with age, my horror at the cruelty of governments grows greater, and if I did what you want, I should seem to hold one form of government more responsible than the other, and that would betray my convictions. Communist, fascist, nationalist, clerical, anti-clerical, are all responsible according to the number of victims. I have not been silent; I have used the only vehicle I possess—verse. If you have my poems by you, look up a poem called "The Second Coming." It was written some sixteen or seventeen years ago and foretold what is happening. I have written of the same thing again and

> again since. This will seem little to you with your strong practical sense, for it takes fifty years for a poet's weapons to influence.[24]

People have defended Yeats but what I feel is that he should have tried to save Ossietsky's life, at least, on humanitarian grounds. Sometimes we break our principles or make deviations from our norms when we want to save an innocent man's life; Gandhiji made similar mistake, but really very serious, when he refused to save Sardar Bhagat Singh's life. Yeats should have recommended Ossietisky for Nobel Prize to save his life from the cruel Nazis; it was another matter whether Hitler would release him or not.

In the middle of the nineteen-thirties the situation of the world, especially the western world, worsened and people began to doubt the efficacy of the League of Nations. Yeats, too, seriously viewed the future of mankind with a growing gloominess. He suspected the motives of the political leaders. What he had envisioned in *A Vision* was now coming to reality. In "The Second Coming" it was the image of the destructive forces in the form of a strange beast slouching towards Bethlehem to be born; now the beast is born to destroy the whole world. The main problem in Yeats's last poems is how to save mankind and all its wonderful works in this crisis ridden world.

The volume *Last Poems* opens with "The Gyres." Confronted with the present tragedy and the loss of all priceless things, symbols of civilization, the poet takes solace in the Nietzschean philosophy of tragic joy:

> Irrational streams of blood are staining earth;
> Empedocles has thrown all things about;
> Hector is dead and there's a light in Troy;
> We that look on but laugh in tragic joy. (*C.P.* 337)

But as the title suggests the outlook is not entirely Nietzschean. In *A Vision* Yeats explains the rise and fall of civilizations in terms of the movements of the gyres which expand and recede alternately:

> Conduct and work grow coarse, and coarse the soul,
> What matter? Those that Rocky Face holds dear,

Lovers of horses and of women, shall,
From marble of a broken sepulchre,
Or dark betwixt the polecat and the owl,
Or any rich, dark nothing disinter
The workman, noble and saint, and all things run
On that unfashionable gyre. (*C.P.* 337)

This theme is taken in one of his greatest poems, "Lapis Lazuli." The question is: when the horror of annihilation has made man hopeless, what solution a poet or artist has to offer? The solution that Yeats offers is the tragic joy, the acceptance of the cycle of history, of running of the gyres and that with the death of a civilization there is the birth of another civilization and artists create the new civilization. The poem begins with the complaint of the "hysterical women" expressed in the poet's words:

They are sick of the palette and fiddle-bow,
Of poets that are always gay
For everybody knows or else should know
That if nothing drastic is done
Aeroplane and zeppelin will come out,
Pitch like King Billy bomb-balls in
Until the town lie beaten flat. (*C.P.* 338)

The poet takes the complaint lightly. This is evidenced by the use of words like "hysterical," "zeppelin," "pitch," "King Billy" and "bomb-balls." He knows the truth of the progress of history, the nature of tragedy and the artist's role in a tragic situation. He meditates on the tragic characters of Shakespeare in the second stanza and concludes that all people have to face tragedy and, so, should accept it stoically:

All perform their tragic play,
There struts Hamlet, there is Lear,
That's Ophelia, that Cordelia;
Yet they, should the last scene be there,
The great stage curtain about to drop,
If worthy their prominent part in the play,
Do not break up their lines to weep. (*C.P.* 338)

Developing the idea further in the subsequent lines of the stanza, he says that tragedy cannot grow more even if we weep or rage to our utmost and, therefore, we should remain gay:

Though Hamlet rambles and Lear rages,
And all the drop-scenes drop at once
Upon a hundred thousand stages,
It cannot grow by an inch or ounce. (*C.P.* 338)

The horizon expands in the third stanza; the vision shifts from the individuals to the tragedy of civilizations:

On their own feet they came, or on shipboard
Camel-back, horse-back, ass-back, mule-back
Old civilizations put to the sword. (*C.P.* 338)

Nothing remains. Every civilization meets its tragic end. In "Meditations in Time of Civil War" there is remorse for the loss of ingenious beautiful things; here the attitude is philosophical:

No handiwork of Callimachus,
Who handled marble as if it were bronze,
Male draperies that seemed to rise
When sea-wind swept the corner, stands;
His long lamp-chimney shaped like the stem
Of a slender palm, stood but a day;
All things fall and are built again
And those that build them again are gay. (*C.P.* 339)

Poets and artists are builders of civilization. Since they know that every civilization must come to its end, that every work of art must perish some day and that they have to build civilization again, they remain gay. The two chinamen seated on the top of a hill view the present tragic scene and, when asked to play sad music, they play expertly but they themselves remain unaffected by the tragedy taking place before them:

There, on the mountain and the sky,
On all the tragic scene they stare.
One asks for mournful melodies;
Accomplished fingers begin to play,
Their eyes mid many wrinkles, their eyes
Their ancient eyes, glittering eyes, are gay. (*C.P.* 339)

The other important element in Yeats's last poems is "Irishry." He loved all those Irishmen who did something for the country. Since England had ruled Ireland for a long time and persecuted a large number of the Irish patriots, he hated the empire and the imperialists. Hone describes a talk between Lady Wellesley and W.B. Yeats:

> Lady Gerald Wellesley reproached him for encouraging hate between two nations. He replied that he was shocked by her thought. 'How could I hate England, owing what I do to Shakespeare, Blake and Morris? England is the only country I cannot hate.' But she herself, at the end of her book, refers to his frequent anti-English outbursts.[25]

Hone simply describes the event but does not explain Yeats's true feelings. Yeats was not against the English in his later age; on the other hand, he had a number of friends. What he hated was the British government. He disliked from the core of his heart the machinations of the rulers and even after independence did not forget them. So when he read Dr. Malony's book on the forged diaries of Roger Casement he grew angry. He wrote to Ethel Mannin:

> I am in a rage, I have just got a book published by the Talbot Press called *The Forged Casement Diaries.* It is by a Dr. Malony I know in New York and he has spent years collecting evidence. He proved that the diaries, supported to prove Casement 'a Degenerate' and successfully used to prevent an agitation for his reprieve, were forged. Casement was not a very able man but he was gallant and unselfish, and had surely his right to leave what would have been considered an unsullied name. I long to break up my rule against politics and call these men criminals but I must not. Perhaps a verse may come to me, now or a year later.[26]

Two poems came out of the rage. The first poem "Roger Casement" is a defence of the man* that he actually was a guiltless man and that his diaries, proving him to be a homosexual, were forged to defame him:

---

* Roger Casement, the British Consular agent in Germany, was charged with treason by the British government and was hanged in 1916. In fact, he was planning to send ammunitions to help the Easter rebels. The British government got scent of his plan. He was arrested, prosecuted and sentenced to death by hanging. Lest the Irish people would agitate, the British government published forged diaries to malign him.

Come Tom and Dick, come all the troop
That cried it far and wide,
Come from the forgerer and his desk
Desert the perjurer's side;
Come speak your bit in public
That some amends be made
To this most gallant gentleman
That is in quick-lime laid. (*C.P.* 352)

This poem is rather mild, but the other poem. "The Ghost of Roger Casement" having the refrain—"The Ghost of Roger Casement/Is beating on the door—is violent and attacking. Here Yeat's hate of the rulers has burst out with all force:

John Bull has stood for Parliament,
A dog must have his day,
The country thinks no end of him,
For he knows how to stay
At a bean feast or a banquet,
That all must hang their trust
Upon the British Empire
Upon the Church of Christ. (*C.P.* 353)

The irony underlying the last two lines is subtle but sharp-cutting. In the next stanza reference to India indictates that the cunningness of the imperialists is not confined to Ireland only:

John Bull has gone to India
And all must pay him heed
For histories are there to prove
That none of another breed
Has had a like inheritance
Or sucked such milk as he. (*C.P.* 353)

The concluding stanza exhorts the Irish people to shout in favour of Roger Casement:

Come round, beloved and bitter men,
Draw round and raise a shout;
The Ghost of Roger Casement
Is beating on the door. (*C.P.* 353)

Yeats's nationalism is discernible in "The O'Rahilly," "Come, Gather Round Me Parnellites" and "Three Songs to the One Burden." His aim in writing these poems is to revive the memory of the forgotten nationalists and their ideas. The O'Rahilly was one of the leaders killed in the Easter Rising. Unfortunately, he was not counted as one of the great martyrs by Yeats. Here in this poem he corrects himself. He wants the honorific "The" to be added to his name because he was a true Irishman* and his family always had this honorific:

> Sing of the O'Rahilly,
> Do not deny his right;
> Sing a 'the' before his name
> Allow that he, despite
> All those learned historians,
> Established it for good. (*C.P.* 354)

The second stanza is devoted to his heroism and association with Pearse and Connolly:

> Sing of the O'Rahilly
> That had such little sense
> He told Pearse and Connolly
> He'd gone to great expense
> Keeping all the Kerry men
> Out of the crazy fight. (*C.P.* 354)

The third stanza continues the same idea:

> Then on Pearse and Connolly
> He fixed a bitter look:
> 'Because I helped to wind the clock
> I come here to strike.' (*C.P.* 354)

The concluding stanza is a homage to the young man.

> What remains to sing about
> But of the death he met
> Stretched under a doorway
> Somewhere off Henry Street;
> They that found him found upon
> The door above his head
> 'Here died the O'Rahilly.
> RIP' writ in blood. (*C.P.* 355)

What gives permanence to this poem is the change in tone from the casual to the tragic and the refrain that changes its meaning

* It was customary among the Irish noble men to add "the" before their names.

in each stanza. The first stanza moves briskly in a lighter vein. But the refrain with its hidden irony prepares us for something serious to come. The refrain in the second stanza is a kind of commentary that reminds us of the fact that the present generation has forgotten its past heroes like the O'Rahilly. The last stanza moves with a quick pace in the beginning but after describing O'Rahilly's death drags on heavily and the concluding line with the acronym RIP, stressed heavily, stops the emotionally charged breath of the reader:

> Here died the O'Rahilly
> RIP writ in blood.

"Come Gather Round Me Parnellites" is the defence of his ideal hero. The deviation in this poem is that Parnell is not pictured as an aristocrat but as an Irish peasant. Written in the ballad style, but in Ottava Rima his favourite stanza form in all his serious poems, the poem moves majestically all through:

> Stand upright on your legs while,
> Stand upright while you can,
> For soon we lie where he is laid
> And he is underground. (*C.P.* 355)

The reasons for praising the "chosen man" are four: the first is that Parnell fought well against the British government, second that he saved the Irish poor, third that he loved a woman (Mrs. O'Shea) dearly and fourth that he was a proud man. The appeal of the poem lies in its calm dignity and lurking irony. We come to realise the grief of Yeats when we reach the last stanza where betrayal by the church and captain O'Shea is understated:

> The Bishops and the Party
> That tragic story made
> A husband that had sold his wife
> And after that betrayed. (*C.P.* 356)

The third song of the "Three Songs To The One Burden" celebrates the Easter heroes, Pearse and Connolly. It does not and perhaps, its aim is not to, achieve the tragic grandeur of "Easter 1916." It opens in the style of "Come Gather Round Me Parnellites":

> Come gather round me, players all
> Come praise Nineteen-Sixteen. (*C.P.* 373)

But the tone becomes serious:

Those from the pit and gallery
Or from the painted scene
That fought in the Post Office
Or round the City Hall
Praise every man that came again
Praise every man that fell. (*C.P.* 373)

The second stanza describes the heroes' tragic role in the drama of the Easter Rising:

Who was the first man shot that day?
The player Connolly,*
Close to the City Hall he died
Carriage** and voice had he;
He lacked those years that go with skill,
But later might have been
A famous, a brilliant figure
Before the painted scene
From mountain to mountain ride the fierce horsemen.
(*C.P.* 373)

The third and final stanza describes the other heroes and ends with the famous words of Pearse modified. "Bloodshed is a cleansing and sanctifying thing" and it would take "the blood of the sons of Ireland to redeem Ireland":

Some had no thought of victory
But had gone out to die
That Ireland's mind be greater,
Her heart mount up on high;
And yet who knows what's yet to come?
For Patrick Pearse had said
That in every generation
Must Ireland's blood be shed.
From mountain to mountain ride the fierce horsemen.
(*C.P.* 373-74)

---

* James Connolly was wounded and after arrest was brought in a wheel-chair. He said, "You can shoot me if you like but I am dying for my country."

** The word is printed "carriage" but it should be "courage."

By presenting the heroes as characters in a tragedy and using the refrain Yeats links the past with the present and suggests that the spirit of heroism is still there in Ireland.

What can be the possible reason for writing these political ballads? The reason, I think, is that Yeats wanted common people to know the Irish heroes more intimately and retain them in their memory. He was well aware of the fact that his serious and difficult poems would be confined to the intellectual class only and therefore he composed ballads in a simple language to be sung by the folk. Besides, he himself had learnt about the mythical and legendary figures through folk-tales and ballads and so knew the truth that great figures become immortal in legends and folk-tales. He wanted to immortalise Parnell, Pearse, Connolly, Casement and O'Rahilly and so wrote ballads to be sung by peasants and workers.

REFERENCES

1. A. Wade, ed., *The Letters of W.B. Yeats,* 779.
2. *Ibid.,* 779.
3. *Explorations,* 343-44.
4. *Ibid.,* 332.
5. *Ibid.,* 334.
6. *Ibid.,* 335.
7. *Ibid.,* 336.
8. *Ibid.,* 337.
9. *Ibid.,* 351-52.
10. *Ibid.,* 356-57.
11. *Ibid.,* 354.
12. *Ibid.,* 354.
13. *Ibid.,* 356.
14. *Ibid.,* 344-45.
15. *Ibid.,* 345.
16. *Ibid.,* 345-46.
17. *A. Wade,* ed., *The Letters of W.B. Yeats,* 811-12.
18. *Ibid.,* 812-13.
19. A.N. Jeffares, *W.B. Yeats: Man and the Poet,* 278.
20. T.R. Henn, *The Lonely Tower,* 344.
21. C.C. O'Brien, "Passion and Cunning" *In Excited Reverie,* 257.

22. A. Wade, ed., *The Letters of W.B. Yeats*, 812.
23. *Ibid.*, 814.
24. *Ibid.*, 850-51.
25. J. Hone *W.B. Yeats 1865-1939.*
26. A. Wade, ed., *The Letters of W.B. Yeats*, 867.

8

ON THE BOILER

Yeats made his last political statement in the long essay *On the Boiler* (now included in *Explorations* with a few omissions). It is a serious essay tinged with occasional humour, sometimes with jokes at the author himself. The other important work "Under Ben Bulben," a long poem, reflects Yeats's views on poetry, art, politics and life in the most precise words possible. These two works, if read side by side, give us an idea of Yeats's thought-process during the fag end of his life. They also make us admire that even at that period when he was physically very weak he could think deeply and produce a poem of great weight.

On the Boiler begins with the explanation of the title:

> When I was a child and wandering about the Sligo Quays I saw a printed, or was it a painted notice? On such-and-such day 'the great McCoy will speak on the old boiler.' I knew the old boiler, very big, very high, the top far out of reach, and all red rust. I wanted to go and hear him for the boiler's sake, but nobody encouraged me.[1]

McCoy, he continues telling, always defied the commonplace customs and revelled in wrecklessness. This account of the ship's carpenter, perhaps, is one of the myths Yeats was fond of creating. We may say that he is in the line of Red Hanrahan, Michael Robartes, Owen Aherne and Giraldus, all projections of Yeats's self. The poem that follows McCoy's adventure in the boat is really serious and meaningful and, so, we can assume that every word in the essay reveals Yeats's mind. The poem begins with the question "Why should not old men be mad?" and answers it through a set of images. It ends with the explanation:

Young men know nothing of this sort,
Observant old men know it well;
And when they know what old books tell,
And that no better can be had,
Know why an old man should be mad (*C.P.* 388-89)

With this poem ends the section titled "Name." The main body is divided into five sections: Preliminaries, Tomorrow's Revolution, Private Thoughts, Ireland after Revolution and Other Matters. He, at the outset expresses the opinion that politics, at present, is a plaything in the hands of politicians, journalists and the mob. The Irish people, therefore, must look back to their glorious past and evolve a new system that can make them a great and powerful nation.

The subjects of his contention are aristocracy, Irishry, education and literature which, when combined together, form the unity of culture which will create the proper environment for achieving the unity of being. Taking the help of a psychology, which behaviourism will certainly reject, he asserts that it is heredity* that determines man's intelligence and that environment is ineffectual. Giving importance to heredity and inheritance he says that democracy is harmful to Ireland because it treats all people alike and allows the low calibered people to dominate the talented who are few. In his opinion, it was aristocracy that provided the best kind of administration in the eighteenth century and will do so in future. The standard of the Senate has declined in modern times because the Senators are elected:

> As the nominated element began to die out—almost all were old men—the Senate declined in ability and prestige. In its early days some old banker or lawyer would dominate the House....[2]

Pointing out the low-mentality of the elected ministers and their brutal behaviour to their even dearest friends, he denounces the very principle of election. He with great emotion pleads for the rule of aristocracy, although by aristocracy he means roughly the group of the noble-minded and well-merited people:

* In our time Chomoky, the great linguist, has argued that intelligence and language acquisition ability are genetically transmitted.

> I was six years in the Irish Senate; I am not ignorant of politics elsewhere, and on other grounds I have some right to speak. I say to those that shall rule here: 'If ever Ireland seems molten wax, reverse the process of revolution. Do not try to pour Ireland into any political system. Think first how many able men with public minds the country has, how many it can hope to have in the future, and mould your system upon those men. It does not matter how you get them, but get them. Republics, Kingdoms, Soviets. Corporates, Parliaments are trash.... These men, whether six or six hundred, are the core of Ireland, are Ireland itself.'[3]

He contrasts "Irishry" with the general trait of the English and observes that while the Irish are subjective, the English are objective. Irishry consists of the noble and heroic qualities of the best men (both Protestant and Catholic) of Ireland. He says:

> I write with two certainties in mind: first that a hundred men, their creative power wrought to the highest pitch, their will trained in war or peace, than a million of any lesser sort no matter how expensive their education, and that although the Irish masses are vague and excitable because they have not yet been moulded and cast, we have a good blood as there is in Europe. Berkeley, Swift, Burke, Grattan, Parnell, Augusta Gregory, Synge, Kevin O'Higgins are the true Irish people, and there is nothing too hard for such as these. If the Catholic names are a few, history will soon fill the gap. My imagination goes back to those Catholic exiled gentlemen of whom Swift said that their bravery exceeded that of all nations.[4]

The poem "The Municipal Gallery Revisited," written in Ottava Rima, is a poetic rendering of the ideas in the quoted passage. It opens with a description of the death of Casement and O'Higgins, the men of heroic mould:

> Around me the images of thirty years:
> An ambush; pilgrims at the water-side;
> Casement upon trial, half-hidden by the bars,
> Guarded; Griffith staring in hysterical pride;
> Kevin O'Higgins' countenance that wears
> A gentle questioning look that cannot hide

A soul incapable of remorse or rest
A revolutionary soldier kneeling to be blessed. (*C.P.* 368)

The meaning will be clear if we read Yeats's *A Speech and Two Poems* (1937) part of which A. Norman Jeffares has quoted in the commentary:

> For a long time I had not visited the Municipal Gallery. I went there a week ago and was restored to many friends. I sat down, after a few minutes, overwhelmed with emotion. There were pictures painted by men, now dead, who were once my intimate friends. There were the portraits of my fellow-workers; there was that portrait of Lady Gregory, by Mancini, which John Synge thought the greatest portrait since Rembrandt; there was John Synge himself; there, too, were portraits of our statesmen; the events of the last thirty years in fine pictures: a peasant ambush, the trial of Roger Casement to Lough Derg, event after event: Ireland not as she is displayed in guide books or history, but, Ireland seen because of the magnificent vitality of her painters, in the glory of her passions.[5]

The last sentence explains the following lines of the second stanza:

'This is not,' I say,
'The dead Ireland of my youth, but an Ireland
The poets have imagined, terrible and gay. (*C.P.* 368)

Stanzas III, IV and V are the poets' musings and the quoted prose passage throws light on their meaning. The following lines of *A Speech and Two Poems* quoted by Jeffares give us an idea of the spirit in which the poem was written:

> For the moment I could think of nothing but that Ireland that great pictured song.... In those rooms of the Municipal gallery I saw Ireland in spiritual freedom....[6]

Stanza VI records Yeats's efforts to achieve that freedom by means of poetry:

John Synge, I and Augusta Gregory, thought
All that we did, all that we said or sang
Must come from contact with the soil, from that
Contact everything Antaeus like grew strong (*C.P.* 369)

Finally, Yeats asserts that he is not the lone man in trying to revive the beautiful and happy Ireland; he has had a group of friends:

> You that would judge me, do not judge alone
> This book or that, come to this hallowed place
> Where my friends' portraits hang and look thereon;
> Ireland's history in their lineaments trace;
> Think where man's glory most begins and ends,
> And say my glory was I had such friends. (*C.P.* 370)

Yeats's intention in this stanza and the preceding will be clear if we compare it with a passage in *On the Boiler*:

> As I wrote these words the Abbey Players are finishing a successful American tour. These tours and Irish songs and novels, when they come from a deeper life than their nineteenth century predecessors, are taking the place of political speakers, political organizations, in holding together the twenty scattered millions conscious of their Irish blood. The attitude towards life of Irish writers and dramatists at this moment will have historical importance. The success of the Abbey Theatre has grown out of a single conviction of its founders; I was the spokesman because I was born arrogant and had learnt an artist's arrogance—'Not what you want but what we want—and we were the first modern theatre that said it. I did not speak for John Synge, Augusta Gregory and myself alone, but for all the dramatists of the theatre.[7]

"The Statues" is closely connected with "The Municipal Gallery Revisited;" it, too, attempts to trace Ireland's history in the "lineaments" of the heroic figures, the subjective men, symbolised here by Cuchulain and Pearse the Easter hero. According to Professor B. Rajan the poem is "an attempted fusion of cultural history with Irish nationalism." No one can deny his view-point but what I feel is that the poem is something more than this. In my opinion, the basic idea is that the superiority of art and thought makes a nation great and invincible. The poet, looking at the statues of Buddha made by the Greek artists, meditates upon their measured and, yet, living character. At first, he considers them to have been planned by Pythagoras but soon rejects this idea because he was abstract:

> Pythagoras planned it. Why did the people stare?
> His numbers, though they moved or seemed to move
> In marble or in bronze, lacked character. (*C.P.* 375)

He says in the second stanza:

> No greater than Pythagoras, for the men
> That with a mallet or a chisel modelled these
> Calculations that look but casual flesh, put down
> All Asiatic Vague immensities,
> And not the banks of oars that swam upon
> The many-headed foam at Salamis. (*C.P.* 375)

Here, he is clear that the statues are products of the objective Europe and subjective Asia and thus represent the unity of being. In other words, they were made at the time when the unity of culture reigned. The reference to Buddha in the third stanza leads us to think of the great sage who had attained *nirvana* and who is described in the poem "The Double Vision of Michael Robertes":

> A Buddha, hand at rest,
> Hand lifted up that blest. (*C.P.* 193)

Here Buddha is depicted in the state of enlightenment or the state of Unity of Being:

> One image crossed the many-headed, sat
> Under the tropic shade, grew round and slow,
> No Hamlet thin from eating flies, a fat
> Dreamer of the Middle Ages. Empty eyeballs knew
> That knowledge increases unreality, that
> Mirror on mirror mirrored is all the show,
> When gong and conch declare the hour to bless
> Grimalkin crawls to Buddha's emptiness. (*C.P.* 375)

The "tropic shade" is the *Bodhi* or *bo* tree where Lord Buddha got enlightenment. Yeats explains the reference to the statues of Buddha in his letter to Edith Shackleton:

> In reading the third stanza, remember the influence on modern sculpture and on the great seated Buddha of the sculptors who followed Alexander.[8]

Yeats, here, is referring to the statues of Lord Buddha found in Kandhar, a city of ancient India, but now of Afghanistan, where the Greek and Indian artists worked together and developed the Gandhara style. Grimalkin is the cat which symbolises objectivity and it surrenders to the subjectivity of Buddha who has attained unity of being. The concluding stanza brings us back to the Irish scene:

> When Pearse summoned Cuchulain to his side,
> What stalked through the Post Office? What intellect,
> What calculation, number, measurement, replied?
>
> (*C.P.* 376)

Here Yeats links Pearse with Cuchulain and Buddha together. As said earlier the image of Buddha in "Double Vision of Michael Robertes and the Dancer" is a figure of the fifteenth phase, the phase of the unity of being. The Gandhara art is the ideal blend of the Greek and Indian arts, the first primary or objective and the second antithetical or subjective. The movement of history (we can say cultural history) is from the primary tincture to the antithetical tincture and then back again to the primary resulting in the death of a particular civilization. The movement was from the calculative numbering and measuring Greece of Pythagoras to the vague immensities of Asia. Yeats's intention in this passage can be understood if we compare it with the following passage from *On the Boiler*:

> Europe was not born when Greek Galleys defeated the Persian hordes at Salamis; but when the Doric Studios sent out those broad-backed marble-statues against the multiform, vague expressive Asiatic sea they gave to the sexual instinct of Europe its goal, its fixed type.[9]

He advises the Irish people to seek the unity of being as did Cuchulain in ancient Ireland and Pearse in modern Ireland. To give an optimistic and positive step in that direction he uses the simple present tense in the concluding lines:

> We Irish born into that ancient sect
> But thrown upon this filthy modern tide
> And by its formless spawning fury wrecked,
> Climb to our proper dark, that we may trace
> The lineaments of a plummet measured face.
>
> (*C.P.* 376)

The poems written after "The Statues" do not have the intensity and vigour of the previously written poems. The reason may be that Yeats after reaching seventy had lost a great part of his energy. But it is also surprising that he produced two of his finest poems only a few months before his death. The minor poems reflect his concern for the future of mankind in the backdrop of the weakening position of the League of Nations and the impending Second World War. At home, he found that the Irish leaders did not come upto expectations. He had hoped for a united Ireland culturally rich, an Ireland where the Protestants and the Catholics would work together for her development. It did not happen. Therefore the only way for him was to bank upon his ideals; the trio of aristocracy, peasantry and artists and forging of Ireland into a heroic nation. The later version of "Three Marching Songs" exhorts the Irish people to remember Emmet, Fitzgerald and Tone who gave up everything for Ireland's freedom:

Remember all those renowned generations
They left their bodies to fatten the wolves.
They left their homesteads to fatten the foxes
Fled to far countries, or sheltered themselves
In cavern, crevice or hole,
Defending Ireland's soul. (*C.P.* 377)

But the stanza in italics—"Be still, be still, what can be said?"—is a bitter comment on the conduct of the present day unheroic leaders. The old bard counts the past heroes* and advises the young people to remember the "renowned generations" who were shot dead or hanged to death. But the comment continues:

Be still, be still, what can be said?
My father sang that song,
But time amends old wrong,
And all that's finished let it fade. (*C.P.* 378)

Now the old bard gets irritat d and angrily says:

Fail, and that history turns into rubbish,
All that great past to a trouble of fools;
Those that come after shall mock : O'Donnell,

* Rony O'Donnell (1575-1608), Shane O'Neill (1530-1567) and Hugh O'Neill (1540-1616) were among the first to fight for Irelands freedom.

Mock at the memory of both O'Neills,
Mock Emmet, mock Parnell
All the renown that fell. (*C.P.* 378)

But the response is again indifferent: "Be still...let it fade."

If this poem is bitter and full of remorse for the loss of the heroic days, "The Statesman's Holiday" is a sarcasm aimed at the opportunism of politicians. Completed in 1938 it first appeared in *On the Boiler* without bearing its present title. The following passage preceding the poem explains its intention:

> Here in Monte Carlo, when I am writing somebody talked of a man with a monkey and some kind of stringed instrument, and it has pleased me to imagine him a great politician. I will make him sing to the sort of tune that goes well with my early sentimental poems.[10]

Unterecker in his *Guide* to W.B. Yeats expresses the view that the imagined statesman in the poem is Yeats himself:

> Though his old man is, of course, a fiction, Yeats may have been remembering his own days as a statesman and his experiences in the 'great houses.'[11]

I am concerned here with Yeats's intention underlying the text. His intention is to deride the contemporary politicians and their activities. Just as a *madari* takes a monkey and makes it dance to his tune, the present politicians make the common people dance to their tune. The first four lines of the first stanza, of course, are a recollection of his youth when he was actively engaged in politics:

I lived among great houses,
Riches drove out rank,
Base drove out the better blood
And mind and body shrank. (*C.P.* 389)

But even in these lines bitterness is evident. The next eight lines explain the reason why he abandoned politics and took poetry as his trade:

No Oscar ruled the table,
But I had a troop of friends
That knowing better talk had gone
Talked of odds and ends.

Some knew what ailed the world
But never said a thing,
So I have picked a better trade
And night and morning sing. (*C.P.* 389)

The second stanza is a clear derision of politicians, where allusions are made to Birkenhead, "Lord Chancellor," Sir Hubert Gough, "Commanding Officer that tore/The Khaki from his back," De Valera, George II, "King of Greece," and Lord Nuffied, "the man that made motors." They are all imaged as a *madari* with a monkey, playing a fiddle:

Ach, call me what you please!
Here's a Montenegrin lute,
And its old sole string
Makes me sweet music
And I delight to sing. (*C.P.* 389)

"Politics," too, is written in the same satirical vein but with an emphasis on youth and love. The poem has the superscription "In our time the destiny of man presents its meaning in political terms," which is a quotation from Thomas Mann. Yeats's intention in this poem is to convey the idea that politics is not everything in life; love is more important than politics. He says in the opening lines of this short poem that it is difficult to listen to talks on the Roman, Russian or Spanish political issues when there is a beautiful girl present before him:

How can I, that girl standing there
My attention fix
On Roman or on Russian
Or on Spanish politics? (*C.P.* 392-93)

He accepts the importance of politics and war in the middle lines:

Yet here's a travelled man that knows
What he talks about,
And there's a politician
That has read and thought,
And may be what they say is true
Of war and war alarms. (*C.P.* 393)

In the concluding lines he rejects the privacy of politics and of war and says:

But O that I were young again
And held her in my arms! (*C.P.* 393)

It follows that youth and love are the governing principles of life, not politics and war.

"The Black Tower" was completed on 21 January, 1939 just seven days before his death. But we should consider "Under Ben Bulben" his last poem as Yeats intended it to be. The definitive edition published by Macmillan ends with "Under Ben Bulben." Therefore we shall consider "The Black Tower" first. The best interpretation of this poem has been made by C.M. Bowra in *Poetry and Politics* and I will closely follow his argument.

The tower, black and hence ancient, is the last support in this troubled world and it must be defended, though its men are weak, old and poor:

Say that the men of the old black tower,
Though they but feed as the goatherd feeds,
Their money spent, their wine gone sour,
Lack nothing that a soldier needs,
That all are oath-bound men,
Those banners come not in. (*C.P.* 396)

They are hand-pressed in the troubled situation and yet are fully determined to defend it from the invaders as they know that it is the ancient tradition, here symbolised by the black tower, alone that can save people from the disintegrating disaster. They are resolute not to be taken in by modern political propaganda; they are fully convinced that the present day war-mongering politicians are enemies of the rich Irish tradition. They are committed to their ideology and will not give in to any kind of pressure, bribe or threat:

Those banners come to bribe or threaten,
Or whisper that man's a fool
Who, when his own right king's forgotten,
Cares what king sets up his rule. (*C.P.* 396)

The atmosphere grows dark in the concluding stanza:

The tower's old cook that must climb and clamber
Catching small birds in the dew of the morn

When we hale men lie stretched in slumber
Swears that he hears the king's great horn.
But he's a lying hound:
Stand we on guard oath-bound!

The defenders of the tower disbelieve the old cook who says that he has heard the king's horn. They know how king Arthur was beguiled when an ignorant man cut his garter, thinking that he had heard the sound of the mythical bugle. Here the ignorant cook is called a lying hound because no one has heard the horn. The inmates, therefore, decide to stand on guard. C.M. Bowra comments:

> The 'Black Tower' marks the end of an epoch, which had indeed kept much that was worth keeping from the past and was threatened with incalculable changes. The struggle which he depicted in this enigmatic form could be interpreted in many ways, but in all of them what counts is the conviction that human dignity is in danger and can be saved only by being true to itself.[12]

Yeats's political poetry, or even the poems dealing with other themes, written after 1935 is a defence of his cherished ideals but it lacks the intensity and strength of his middle years. The main reason may be his bad health and shattering of his dreams. The other reason may be that he was exerting all his energy on "Under Ben Bulben" which may be called his testament and which certainly is one of his masterpieces.

Divided into six sections and each section defining an independent notion, the poem encompasses man in his entirety. The first section opens in the typical Yeatsian way:

Swear by what the sages spoke
Round the Mareotic Lake
That the Witch of Atlas knew,
Spoke and set the cocks a, crow. (*C.P.* 397)

The juxtaposition of "the sages" (perhaps of Sailing to Byzantium) and Shelley's Witch of Atlas makes it clear that the poet is in trance and is going to deliver their wisdom before the reader. The next stanza refers to the aristocrats of the past, both men and women, and the fairies of Ben Bulben:

Swear by those horsemen, by those women
Complexion and form prove superhuman,
That pale long visaged company
That air in immortality
Completeness of their passions won;
Now they ride the wintry dawn
Where Ben Bulben sets the scene. (*C.P.* 397-98)

The third stanza of the section is only one line. This device of distancing it from the rest is for the sake of emphasis:

Here's the gist of what they mean.

Section II describes the antinomies, vascillations, the different incarnations and rebirth. First the antinomies and vascillation:

Many times man lives and dies
Between his two extremeties,
That of race and that of soul
And ancient Ireland knew it all. (*C.P.* 398)

And later on he speaks of soul's immortality:

Though grave digger's toil is long,
Sharp their spades, their muscles strong
They but thrust their buried men
Back in the human mind again. (*C.P.* 398)

The third section is rather biographical. Once an admirer of Mitchel, Yeats quotes his slogan, an adaptation of a line from the New Testament, and says violence is a part of life; a wise man must be a man of action:

Even the wisest man grows tense
With some sort of violence
Before he can accomplish fate,
Knows his work or choose his mate. (*C.P.* 398-99)

The fourth section treats the theme of perfection in art and poetry. His first advice is to follow the tradition created by great artists.

Poet and sculptor, do the work,
Nor let the modish painter shirk
What his great forefathers did,
Bring the soul of man to God
Make him fill the cradles right. (*C.P.* 399)

Then he refers to the Egyptian art, the art of Phidias and Michael Angelo who believed in the balance of flesh and spirit. The Irish people, like Michael Angelo, should know the great truth: "Profane perfection of mankind." The artists who followed Angelo are Quattro Cent Calvert, Wilson, Blake, Claude and Palmer but now the great age has passed and confusion is prevailing upon our thought:

Section V is an advice to the Irish poets:

Irish poets, learn your trade,
Sing whatever is well made,
Scorn the sort now growing up
All out of shape from toe to top. (*C.P.* 400)

Finally, he advises them to sing of the happy people, always capable of producing sweetness and harmony:

Sing the lords and ladies gay
That were beaten into the clay
Through seven heroic centuries;
Cast your mind on other days
That we in coming days may be
Still the indomitable Irishry. (*C.P.* 400)

The poem ends with a rare calm and peace of mind. The violent bitter, passionate aristocrat understands the meaning of life and also of death that it is man's creation. The final section is an epitaph, short and pithy, but speaks volumes on the ideal attitude to life and death:

Under bare Ben Bulben's head
In Drumcliff churchyard Yeats is laid
An ancestor was rector there
Long years ago, a church stands near,
By the road an ancient cross.
No marble, no conventional phrase;
On limestone quarried near the spot
By his command these words are cut:

Cast a cold eye
On life, on death
Horseman, pass by!

REFERENCES

1. *Explorations,* 407.
2. *Ibid.*, 412-13.
3. *Ibid.*, 414.
4. *Ibid.*, 441-42.
5. A.N. Jeffares, *A Commentary on the Poem of W.B. Yeats,* 482-83.
6. *Ibid.*, 483.
7. *Explorations,* 414-15.
8. A. Wade, ed., *The Letters of W.B. Yeats,* 911.
9. *Explorations,* 451.
10. *Ibid.*, 252.
11. John Unterecker, *A Reading Guide to W.B. Yeats,* 287.
12. C.M. Bowra, *Poetry and Politics,* 50-51.

Conclusion

Yeats's poetical development is basically shaped by the politics of his time and refutes the validity of the maxim "art for art's sake." He, of course, began writing poetry in Arcadia and under the influence of the romantics and the aesthetic developed the theory that poetry should be about beautiful things and soft feelings. Naturally, his early poetry is an aspiration for the land of heart's desire and is partly tinged with an escapist tone. If he had not come in contact with the nationalists of his time and actively involved himself in Irish politics he would have become another Morris or Wilde or Dowson.

The seed of nationalism that was sown in his early boyhood sprouted forth and developed into a strong tree when he came in contact with John O'Leary and the literary works of Davis Mangan, William Allingham and Standish O'Grady. The problem before him was how to load the dreamy language of his time with the stern reality of current social, political and cultural problems and develop a new poetics. He began to form a group of writers who would support him in his new endeavour, the endeavour to elevate the Irish literature that would be an integrating factor in the Irish life and compete well with other literatures of the world, especially those of France and England. Ireland, he sincerely felt, had a glorious past but the dark shadow of the British empire eclipsed all its brightness. Therefore, it was the duty of every Irishman to free the nation politically and culturally from England and this could be done most fruitfully by reviving Ireland's old spirit by means of literature and Irish nationalism. Yeats combined nationalism with poetry to make Ireland a great nation. Consequently, he began writing poetry on Irish myths legends, folk-tales and ancient history and advised his compatriots to use Irish materials in their poetry. He founded the Irish Literary Society in London first and then in Dublin and at other places, lectured at various literary clubs, and, later on, launched the ambitious Irish Dramatic Movement. All these activities, the bitter-sweet experiences, and contact with different kinds of people, made him a realist and rooted in the native soil firmly and changed him from a dreamer to the practical visionary. Now he was able to make a beautiful blend of romanticism and realism.

The controversies over the publication of books, estrangement in love, riots over syngis and his own plays, the hostility of the church and the court case and arrest of his players in America seasoned him to face the challenges of life. As his attitude to life changed, he gave up the old dreaminess, vagueness, weariness, languor and melancholy note of his early poetry and began to write a different kind of poetry marked by terseness, precision, complexity and plainness. He broke away from the French symbolist tradition in the Hugh Lane poems. The French symbolists used private symbols which needed some explanation but Yeats made the public men symbols of his ideas.

In the Easter poems where he admires the martyrdom of Pearse, Connolly, McBride, McDonagh and Con Markiewicz, he made a new use of symbols. The fact is that the Hugh Lane poems mark the beginning of a new kind of poetry, modern and Yeatsian, public and yet private, realistic but prophetic. What is more significant is the ancient legendary and mythical figures—Conchubar, Cuchulain, Fergus, Aengus Deirdre and the fairies—are replaced by historical characters like Wolfe Tone, Robert Emmet, Edward Fitzgerald, Charles Parnell, John O'Leary, Padraic Pearse, James Connolly and people of his own circle. In fact, these people become a part of his mythology.

Yeats hoped that the heroic deeds and noble sacrifice of the Easter martyrs would integrate Ireland emotionally and unify the Irish people politically but the events after 1916 belied his hope. The reprisals of the Black and Tans, cruelty on both the British and the Irish sides, the Civil War that followed the Treaty, the growing uncertainty in world politics and the aftermath of the First World War made him unhappy and meditative and the old fire that had kindled his spirit began to fade.

Irelands' independence in 1921 and his nomination to the Senate by Cosgrave's government revived his spirit and he felt that he would do something for the country. In fact, he did justice to his new assignment; his speeches on education, divorce and Ireland's future were original and of immense value but the bitterness between the political factions, one led by De Valera and the other by Griffith and after his death by Cosgrave frustrated his plans.

Bitter and frustrating experiences of active politics impelled him to look for a philosophy that would explain the nature of events and the course of history and provide a sound base of his poetry. He had developed the concepts of Unity of Culture, Unity of Being, the individual memory and the racial memory in the early days of his occultism. Now his problem was to place all these concepts in the historical perspective. After a study of Hegel, Nietschze, Schopenhauer, Vico, Frazer and Toynbee he gave his own interpretation of the movement of history. He was concerned with not only the society and state but also the individual; for him both were of equal importance. Unless there was Unity of Culture, Unity of Being was not possible. To widen his world outlook he studied the Upanishads and Buddhism deeply. He rejected Karl Marx partly on the ground that the great philosopher was a materialist (of course, he was wrong in his opinion and should have read Marx's philosophical writings in Original). He summarised his idea of the progress of history in terms of the rise and fall of civilizations in a cyclical order and of the individual, in the same manner, like the phases of the moon. His interpretation of the progress of the individual and civilization is partly mythical and partly historical. What is significant is that it fills us with hope in the utmost tragic situation.

Now the question arises, how far was Yeats successful in his political poems? Did the political ideas and themes, so dominant in the poetry, narrow his vision and dilute the intensity of feeling? Or to put in other words, is his poetry dealing with political issues or inspired by politics partisan and ephemeral or propagandist in nature? The answer is, as I have ventured to give, that he enriched modern poetry by making it contemporary and real. Engels had said that he had learnt more from Balzac about the French society than from the historians; we too know more about Ireland of Yeats's time from his creative writing. One of the important aims of poetry is, no doubt, to give the reader aesthetic pleasure. But what is more important is that it should present reality truthfully, defend human values artistically, envision a society where people can live a better life. The greatness of Yeats's poetry is that it interprets the contemporary political events within the framework of a philosophical system.

Finally, which is more important, politics or poetry? For Yeats, poetry is more important than politics. Politics determines a man's place in the body politic, whether he is a member of a tribal group or a developed society. But all politics is determined by man's economic activities and the relation between productive forces, tools of production and mode of production. Poetry, although a part of superstructure, is an expression of man's consciousness which is ever changing and ever progressing. Minor poets express their individual and class consciousness and, as such, never rise above their class interest. Great poets speak for all people and rise above the petty politics of their class. In other words they cross the boundary of politics and enter the higher realm of philosophy. Thus their poetry is neither propagandist nor ephemeral; on the other hand it is universal and permanent. Yeats always rose above the ephemerality of politics and attempted at achieving permanence in poetry by following a philosophical system. Born in a Protestant Anglo-Irish family he could easily have gone to the English side. But he chose to represent the repressed Irish people. He was a nationalist, no doubt, but he spoke for all the nations colonised by the British people. He had a special sympathy for India and her people. As a poet he was concerned with human values. He argued that there should be a proper balance between matter and spirit. Spirit is more important but it has its proper place in the body. Since politics deals basically with the material aspect of life, it has its own importance. It provides the material base of poetry. Aristotle said that a work of art is a synodal, a concretum of the form and matter; a statue is neither a piece of marble nor the human body but a work of art. Yeats used the political events but philosophised them to make his poetry have universal appeal.

We may not entirely agree with his political ideas especially his love of aristocracy, flirtation with fascism, hatred of democracy but we cannot say that he was against humanity. The great drawback in his philosophical system is his interpretation of history. History progresses dialectically and never returns to its previous stages. The causes of historical progress are man's material activities which determine the progress of ideas. Inspite of these drawbacks and limitations, Yeats is the greatest poet of the twentieth century and ranks with the greatest poets of the world. He never shirked from the harsh realities of time. A nationalist, an active politician, an occultist and a poet he envisioned a world where man can achieve the unity of being. Not only this, he showed the way to achieve it.

SELECTED BIBLIOGRAPHY

PRIMARY SOURCES

The Collected Poems of W.B. Yeats. London: Macmillan, 1950.

Autobiographies. London: Macmillan, 1956.

The Collected Plays of W.B. Yeats. London: Macmillan, 1952.

A Vision. London: Macmillan, 1937.

Alt, Peter, and Russell K. Alpach, ed., *The Variorun Edition of W.B. Yeat's Poetry*. New York: Macmillan, 1957.

Mythologies. London: Macmillan, 1959.

Essays and Introductions. London: Macmillan, 1961.

Explorations. London: Macmillan, 1962.

Letters on Poetry from W.B. Yeats to Dorothy Welleshey. London: OUP, 1940.

Wade, A. *The Letters of W.B. Yeats*: London: Rupert Hart-Davis, 1954.

Skelton, R. and David R. Clark, ed., *W.B. Yeats: The Irish Renaissance*. Dublin: Dolmen Press London: OUP, 1965.

Unterecker, John, ed., *W.B. Yeats and Patrick McCarton: A Fenian Friendship*. Dublin: Dolmen Press, 1965. Distributors OUP.

Frayne, John P., ed., *The Uncollected Prose of W.B. Yeats* Vol. I. London: Macmillan, 1970.

Frayne, John P. and Colton Johnson, ed. *The Uncollected Prose of W.B. Yeats*. London: Macmillan, Vol. I, 1970, Vol. II, 1975.

Mikhail, E.H., ed. *W.B. Yeats: Interviews and Recollections*, Vol. I and II. London: Macmillan, 1977.

Donoghus, Dennis, ed., *Memoirs*. London: Macmillan, 1988.

BIOGRAPHIES

Hone, J. *W.B. Yeats* 1865-1939 2nd ed. London: Macmillan, 1962.

Macrae, Alsadair D.F., *W.B. Yeats: A Literary Life*. London: Macmillan, 1994.

SECONDARY SOURCES

Bowra, C.M. *The Heritage of Symbolism*. London: Macmillan, 1963.

——. *Poetry and Politics*. London: CUP, 1965.

Bjersby, Birgit. *The Cuchulain Legends in the Works of W.B. Yeats*. Upsala, 1950.

Bloom, H. *W.B. Yeats*. London: OUP, 1970.

Bradford, C. *Yeats at Work*. New York: Southern Illinois UP, 1965.

Cullingforth, E. *Yeats, Ireland and Fascism*. New York: New York UP, 1981.

Donoghue Dennis. *Yeats*. London: Fontana, 1971.

Ellmann, R. *W.B. Yeats: Man and the Masks*. London: Macmillan, 1949.

——. *The Identity of Yeats*. London: OUP, 1954.

Ellis-Fermor, Una. *The Irish Dramatic Movement*. London: Methuen, 1957.

Fallis, R. *The Irish Renaissance*. New York: Syracuse UP, 1977.

Ferrall, Charles. *Modernist Writing and Reactionary Politics*. London: CUP, 2001.

Faulkner, Peter. *Yeats and the Irish 18th Century*. Dublin: Dolmen Press, 1965.

Fraser, G.S. *Vision and Rhetoric*. London: Faber and Faber, 1950.

Gibbon, M. *The Masterpiece and the Man*. London: Rupert Hart-Davis, 1955.

Grene, Nicholas. *The Politics of Irish Drama*. London: CUP, 2000.

Hall, J. and M. Steinmann, ed. *The Permanence of W.B. Yeats*. London: Macmillan, 1950.

Henn, T.R. *The Lonely Tower*. Rev. ed. London: Methuen, 1965.

——. *Yeats and the Poetry of War*. London: OUP, 1964.

Hough, Graham. *The Last Romantics*. London: Gerald Duckworth & Co., 1949.

Howes, Marjorie. *Yeats's Nations.* London: CUP, 2001.

Jeffares, A.N. *W.B. Yeats: Man and the Poet.* London: Routledge and Kegan Paul, 1962.

——. *A Commentary on the Poetry of W.B. Yeats.* London: Macmillan, 1970.

——. *A New Commentary on the Poetry of W.B. Yeats.* London: Macmillan, 1984.

——. *The Circus Animals.* London: Macmillan, 1970.

Jeffares, A.N. and K.G.W. Cross, ed. *In Excited Reverie,* London: Macmillan, 1965.

Knights, L.C. *Explorations.* London: Chatto and Windus, 1946.

Kirby, Sheelah, *The Yeats Country.* Dublin : Dolmen Press, 1962.

MacNiece, Louis. *The Poetry of W.B. Yeats.* London: OUP, 1941.

Menon, V.K.N. *The Development of William Butler Yeats,* Edinburgh: Oliver and Boyd, 1942.

Malins. *Yeats and the Easter Rising.* Dublin: Dolmen Press, 1964.

O'Connor, Frank: *The Backward Look.* London: Macmillan, 1965.

Rajan, B. *W.B. Yeats. A Critical Introduction.* London: Hutchinson Univ. Library, 1965.

Smith, Stan. *W.B. Yeats: A Critical Introduction.* London: Macmillan, 1990.

Stallworthy, J. *Between the Lines.* London: OUP, 1963.

——. *Vision and Revision of Yeats's Last Poetry,* London: OUP, 1969.

——. ed. *Yeats's Last Poems.* London: Macmillan, 1968.

Stanfield, P.S. *Yeats and Politics in the 1930s.* London: Macmillan, 1988.

Stewart, JIM. *Eight Modern Writers.* London: OUP, 1964.

Stock, A.G. *W.B. Yeats: His Thought and Poetry.* London: CUP, 1961.

Telfer, Giles W.L. *Yeats's Ideal of the Gael.* Dublin: Dolmen Press, 1966.

Unterecker, J. *A Reader's Guide to W.B. Yeats.* London: Thomes and Hudson, 1959.

Ure, Peter. *Towards a Mythology*. London: Holder and Stoughton, 1966.

Zwerdling, A. *Yeats's Idea of Heroic Ireland*. New York: Gerald Duckworth, 1966.

ARTICLES RELATED TO THE TOPIC

Cosgrave, P. "Yeats, Fascism and Conor O'Brien," *London Magazine*, Vol. 7, No. 4, (July 1967).

Daiches, David. "The Practical Visionary," *Encounter*, Vol. XIX, No. 3, (September 1962).

Diskin, Patrick. "A Source for Yeats's 'The Black Tower'" *Notes, and Queries*, Vol. VIII, No. 3, (1961).

Garrab, Arra M. "The Forged Casement Diaries," *English Language Notes*, Vol. II, 1968.

JOURNAL DEVOTED TO YEATS

Yeats Annual. London: Macmillan.